THE ULTIMATE GUIDE TO
STRANGER THINGS

sona
BOOKS

sona
BOOKS

**First published in the UK 2022 by Sona Books
an imprint of Danann Media Publishing Ltd.**

© 2022 Danann Media Publishing Limited

**Images courtesy of
Alamy & Getty Images**

Additional writing by Carolyn McHugh

CAT NO: **SON0546**

ISBN: **978-1-915343-06-2**

Made in UAE.

CONTENTS

8

EERIE INDIANA

HOW A PAIR OF BROTHERS BLENDED SECRET CIA EXPERIMENTS,
A CAST OF RELATIVE UNKNOWNS AND A LOVE OF '80S MOVIES
TO MAKE A SMASH-HIT TV SHOW

The Duffer brothers weren't old enough to watch the movies that inspired their hit Netflix series, *Stranger Things*, when they were released in cinemas. But despite being born in 1984 – the year *after* the show's first season is set – Matt and Ross's childhoods were shaped by the pop culture of a decade they're too young to remember. Growing up in North Carolina, the twins spent their childhoods playing Dungeons & Dragons, and devouring VHS tapes of classics like *The Goonies* and *ET* "on rotation" – enough to form a cinematic memory of an era when the effects-driven blockbuster really came into its own.

"I think when you're first watching and discovering movies, at that magic age of eight to 12, they're very powerful," Matt pointed out before *Stranger Things*' first season aired. "Those movies had a huge impact on a lot of us. It's a world we know and understand – we grew up there."

While the Duffers' affection for '80s movies was far from extraordinary, few choose to channel that passion into a TV series – and even fewer persuade a broadcaster or streaming service to join them on the ride. But Netflix saw the potential in the brothers' tale of, well, strange things going on in a small Indiana town, and gave the show the cherished green light.

Ahead of its 2016 launch, however, there was little to suggest it was about to become one of the most popular TV shows on the planet. The likes of *House of Cards*, *Orange is the New Black* and *Daredevil* had made the industry (and awards ceremonies) take notice of the upstart streaming service, but with *The Crown*, *The Witcher* and *Bridgerton* still to come, Netflix was still looking for a blockbuster smash of *Game of Thrones* proportions. And in an era when recognisable franchises had come to dominate, few would have tipped this unfamiliar story – whose biggest star, Winona Ryder, was no longer a Hollywood A-lister – to capture the zeitgeist.

The eight episodes of season one dropped simultaneously on 15 July 2016, and something magical happened. *Stranger Things* was suddenly the show that *everybody* was talking about – following the death of a supporting character, "Justice for Barb" even became a popular rallying cry online – and the million-dollar question was less about whether you'd watched it, than how quickly you'd binged the whole lot. And while Netflix was traditionally cagey about its viewing figures, there was never any doubt that the Duffers' ode to the '80s had become a blockbuster as big as any of the movies that inspired it.

"I knew it was good, but we had no idea whether people would tune in," producer Shawn Levy said in 2017. "I remember as early as the day after launch, the volume of social media I started seeing was astonishing. Within a week it felt like a wave, and within a month it felt like a tsunami."

"We were just trying to tell a story that we knew we would want to watch," Ross Duffer recalled. "We thought that it would appeal to people like us who were nostalgic for this type of storytelling, but I guess what surprised us the most was that it reached a much broader audience than that. For younger people who aren't necessarily as nostalgic for this type of thing to embrace it like they have was a great surprise."

AMBLIN ALONG

Before *Stranger Things*, little on the Duffers' CV hinted at what was to come. They'd written and directed a little-seen 2015 post-apocalyptic movie called *Hidden* and scripted three episodes of M. Night Shyamalan's own tale of a spooky town, *Wayward Pines*, but they were light years from the A-list until their pilot script attracted Shawn Levy's attention.

Levy was well established in Hollywood thanks to his popular *Night at the Museum* movies – he's since directed *Free Guy* and Netflix's own *The Adam Project* – and, unlike the Duffers, was old enough to remember the '80s the first time around. He saw something special in the story, and would become the third corner of the show's core creative triumvirate.

"I was immediately struck by how propulsively it was

paced," he recalled back in 2017. "I think that's an interesting first impression, given how bingeable it later became. And in spite of its hooky mystery and period setting, it carved really three-dimensional and complex characters, where so many period shows and movies have that kitschy hook without servicing character."

Despite becoming best known for its nostalgia, *Stranger Things* didn't start out as a celebration of the movies of the Duffers' youth. Instead, the twins were looking to tell a story based on the infamous real-life MKUltra programme, where the CIA performed covert experiments in mind control from the 1950s through to the '70s. The influence is clear in the show's Hawkins National Laboratory, where shady scientists use a young girl with telekinetic powers as a test subject, and inadvertently open a door to a frightening parallel world known as the Upside Down.

"Honestly, what started this was us remembering the time

when we believed that the government was doing these shady experiments," Ross Duffer said in 2017. "We were looking at *Altered States* and films like that, and thinking we wanted to go back to that Cold War paranoia. That's originally how the conversation started, and it's what led back to these '80s movies that we fell in love with. It started with this idea [of] whether we believed that events like this could be possible somewhere like small-town America. Then that led us to thinking, 'This is when all of our favourite movies are set!' and all those ideas merged together."

While the Duffers hadn't experienced the '80s first hand, they did have an instinctive feel for what made the movies of the era tick. Primarily influenced by Steven Spielberg and his Amblin Entertainment production company – the outfit behind the suburban family-friendly thrills of *Poltergeist*, *Gremlins*, *The Goonies* and *Back to the Future* – they identified a common "sense of wonder and awe in a setting that is very relatable." The similarities are clear in *Stranger Things*, where a quartet of ordinary pre-teens find themselves experiencing close encounters of the supernatural kind, after one of their number – Will Byers – is pulled into the Upside Down.

"We started looking at these films and thinking what it was about them that made us love them so much," Matt said in 2016. "For us it was the juxtaposition of the ordinary and the extraordinary. We had very ordinary suburban lives, and these films tapped into that. They made us think, 'Oh my God, maybe I'm going to find a treasure map in the attic,' or 'What if we find an alien out in the woods?'"

But the Duffers did something more than simply create a televisual cover version of Amblin's greatest hits. Instead, they displayed a Quentin Tarantino-like skill for magpie-ing ideas from disparate – and sometimes surprising – sources. Will's disappearance, for example, has echoes of the abduction of Laura Palmer in David Lynch's *Twin Peaks*, while the twins found inspiration in darker, more grown-up fare from the back catalogues of Stephen King and body horror pioneer David Cronenberg. The fingerprints of John Carpenter, director of *Halloween* and *The Thing*, are also visible throughout – not least in the show's evocative synth score by Kyle Dixon and Michael Stein.

"When we were first pitching the series around we made

Above: The Duffer hive mind in action – Ross and Matt call the shots on Stranger Things' first season

Left: David Harbour was arguably best known for a bit part in *Quantum of Solace* before playing Hawkins' beloved police chief Jim Hopper

a demo reel where we took all these different movies that have inspired us – the Carpenter stuff, the Spielberg stuff – and we scored it with John Carpenter music," Ross Duffer revealed in 2016. "When we put the theme music over *ET*, not only did we realise that it worked but it gave it this exciting edge."

ONCE YOU POP, YOU CAN'T STOP

In hindsight, tapping a wave of nostalgia as *Stranger Things* did seems something of a no-brainer. The show landed on Netflix within a year of the unashamedly retro *The Force Awakens* – a film precision engineered to remind *Star Wars* fans why they fell in love with the saga in the first place – and over the last year, *Ghostbusters:*

BELOW: *Stranger Things* gave Winona Ryder her best role in years, as a mother desperately searching for her son, Will

12

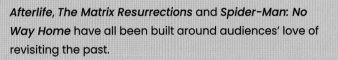

Afterlife, *The Matrix Resurrections* and *Spider-Man: No Way Home* have all been built around audiences' love of revisiting the past.

But there was more to *Stranger Things*' success than timing. Indeed, future *The Force Awakens* director JJ Abrams had ventured into similar territory in 2011 with *Super 8*, but his own love letter to Spielberg – about a bunch of kids whose efforts to make a movie unwittingly record an alien escaping a train crash – was a more modest hit. It also lacked the multi-generational appeal that *Stranger Things* has in abundance, an ability to draw in a generation for whom phones with wires come from a world even more alien than the Upside Down.

"The [best '80s films] don't feel '80s, they feel timeless," Matt Duffer said of the show's era in 2016. "You show a kid one now and nothing feels '80s about it. That was something we were conscious of. It was important that nothing felt too kitschy. Sure, there's a Millennium Falcon toy there and an *Evil Dead* poster here, but it would have been the same style and music if we were shooting a show in 2016."

The Duffers also displayed a very modern instinct for storytelling, exploiting Netflix's all-in-one-go release strategy with cliffhangers that made you desperate to binge the next episode straight away – the televisual equivalent of Pringles' "once you pop, you can't stop" slogan.

"I guess we wrote it and tried to structure it as much as possible like a big eight-hour movie," Matt Duffer admitted ahead of season two. "The cool thing about Netflix is you could spread it out and do one episode a week – though I think we try to make it as hard as possible for you to do that, as we tend to end on these cliffhangers.

"That kind of came about by accident. We always liked having a little teaser leading into the main titles, because we always wanted the opening of the episode to give you a little bit of a rush, and in order to do that it ended up that we would cut out the climax from the episode before and put it into the beginning of the next episode. It was not designed to drive binge-viewing, but I think that it did end up doing that!"

> "They displayed a Quentin Tarantino-like skill for magpie-ing ideas from disparate – and sometimes surprising – sources"

THESE GO TO ELEVEN

Look past the nostalgia, the cliffhangers and the freaky parallel world, however, and arguably the biggest reason for *Stranger Things'* phenomenal success is its characters and the actors who play them – after all, unleashing Demogorgons on an unsuspecting small town counts for nothing if you don't care about the people in harm's way.

It's perhaps appropriate that a show so steeped in Amblin lore should have displayed such a Spielbergian knack for picking child actors, and the four boys at the centre of the story – Mike (Finn Wolfhard), Lucas (Caleb McLaughlin), Dustin (Gaten Matarazzo) and Will (Noah Schnapp) – were all natural successors to the Goonies. Perhaps the most important find, though, was Millie Bobby Brown, the young British actor who became the face of the show playing Eleven, the little girl with close-cropped hair whose telekinetic abilities result in characteristic nosebleeds.

But *Stranger Things* was never just about the kids. From the beginning, it seamlessly blended parallel storylines about the teens and the grown-ups caught up in Will's disappearance, providing entry points for every generation clicking through Netflix's navigation screen. So where younger viewers were more likely to get caught up in Mike, Lucas and Dustin's adventures on their improbable, parent-defying quest to rescue their best friend, adults could relate to Joyce's (Winona Ryder)'s palpable grief at the loss of her son – and her belief that she can communicate with him through the walls of her house, even though everyone in the town thinks she's mad.

Along with fellow '80s/'90s veteran Matthew Modine (who played morally dubious laboratory scientist Dr Martin Brenner), Ryder was by some distance the biggest name in a show that was – initially, at least – seriously short on star power.

Of course, that all changed when the show hit the stratosphere, as the stars became seriously hot property in Hollywood, and big enough to headline blockbuster movies: most notably, Millie Bobby Brown has topped the bill in *Godzilla: **King of the Monsters*** and *Enola Holmes*, David Harbour (police chief Hopper) has starred in

Above: Every Amblin-type story needs a villain... Matthew Modine channels MKUltra as dodgy scientist Dr Martin Brenner

Below: She only appeared in a couple of episodes, but Shannon Purser's Barb became the focus of an unlikely fan movement

Below: Whatever *ET* can do, we can do better... Lucas, Dustin and Will fire up the '80s-appropriate bikes in season one

Hellboy and *Black Widow*, and Finn Wolfhard has taken major roles in the *IT* movies and *Ghostbusters: Afterlife*. Even nominal supporting players like Joe Keery – whose elegantly coiffed Steve Harrington has evolved from school bully to comedic powerhouse – are bankable enough to take major roles in the likes of *Free Guy*.

SEQUEL OPPORTUNITIES

Where success leads, sequels tend to follow, and a Halloween-set second season – inventively titled *Stranger Things 2* – arrived little over a year after its predecessor. In the tradition of James Cameron classics *Aliens* and *Terminator 2*, the Duffers upped the ante by expanding the scope and introducing a bigger threat – in this case the colossal Mind Flayer. But they also played around with the formula, to embrace the fact that their young cast were getting older – by the time the third season arrived

in 2019, John Hughes high school movies were just as big an inspiration as all those Amblin classics.

"You have to take [the kids ageing] into account in the narrative," Matt Duffer said ahead of season two. "It's funny, though, that in the story they were normal kids in season one and then they go through this extraordinary thing that's changed them. In a way that's also happened in their real lives, because they were very real kids last year and they went through an extraordinary change when the show came out. Now they're these little celebrities."

Even three years after our last visit, Eleven, Hopper, Joyce, Mike and the rest are characters you still want to hang out with, with that small Indiana town remaining one of the hottest destinations on TV. Not bad for a story born from two brothers' love of VHS tapes from the now-distant past.

THE CHARACTERS

ELEVEN

THE MYSTERIOUS GIRL AT THE SHOW'S CENTRE, ELEVEN HAS BEEN THROUGH MORE IN HER SHORT TIME THAN MOST GO THROUGH IN A LIFETIME

The closest thing that *Stranger Things* has to a protagonist, Eleven (Millie Bobby Brown) – aka 'Jane Hopper' (more on that later) – has, more than any other character in the show, been through the mill.

Taken from her mother as a child (who herself has been experimented on), El was denied all the things children usually take for granted: care, a family, friends – even a name. Her only moniker comes from the number she has tattooed on her arm.

But that's not the worst of it. Frequently experimented on and punished for not cooperating by the sinister Dr Brenner, her first encounter with the Upside Down, when she accidentally opens the gate at Hawkins Lab, provides El with the means to escape. Happily, this leads to her first encounter with friendly normality in the form of Mike, Dustin and Lucas.

Taking her in, they quickly befriend her and hide her in Mike's basement. While helping them look for their missing friend, Will Byers, she experiences some of the things she was missing: friendship, school, Eggo waffles – even love, as hers and Mike's bond proves to be a strong one. Plus, she makes a school bully wet himself. Can't say fairer than that.

Using her powers, she eventually helps rescue Will and destroy the Demogorgon – seemingly sacrificing herself in the process. In reality, she has been transported to the Upside Down, which she quickly escapes from. Eventually being taken in by Hopper, the two form a paternal bond of sorts, although she eventually grows frustrated with his protective nature.

After a road trip to Chicago – encountering her lobotomised mother on the way, where she learns the truth of her origins – she returns to Hawkins, helping to save the day once more, this time from the Mind Flayer, as she's reunited with Mike and the gang.

From here, things take a much brighter turn for El as Hopper ensures her future by having her legally adopted as his daughter, now named Jane Hopper. As a further sweetener, she gets to attend the Snow Ball with Mike, where the two share a kiss.

From there, El quickly begins the transition into a typical teenager – dating Mike, hanging out with her new friend Max, and giving her new dad all manner of worries.

It's not long before the Upside Down resurfaces as a threat once more, however, with even El struggling against the Mind Flayer-possessed Billy Hargrove.

In spite of this, El is still able to help save the day – although tragically, Hopper seemingly dies in the process. Devastated, El is taken in by Joyce Byers, and the two leave for California alongside Jonathan and Will.

Moving to a new school in California brings problems for El and when she fights back against a school bully she is threatened with incarceration in a juvenile penitentiary. Escaping that, and in a move to restore her powers, El works with Dr Brenner again and discovers the truth about the Hawkins Lab. She gets away and then helps to save her friends by 'piggybacking' off Max's mind to prevent Vecna accessing it. But with Hawkins still under attack as the series ends, she still has a lot to do.

MIKE WHEELER

LIVING PROOF THAT AN IN-DEPTH KNOWLEDGE OF DUNGEONS & DRAGONS CAN SAVE LIVES

If there's a character that goes under the radar in *Stranger Things*, it's Mike Wheeler (Finn Wolfhard). While all the plaudits are thrown at the likes of Eleven, Hopper, Dustin and even Steve Harrington, Mike's at the centre of it all, quietly holding everything together.

Really, it's almost his story. It's his best friend who goes missing, and it's he who shelters Eleven when she first shows up. It's almost like Elliott meeting ET, except right from the off it's clear that Mike has feelings for her.

While Mike, Dustin, Lucas and Will have each other, they are nonetheless bullied outsiders. For this reason, Mike immediately empathises with El, and goes to great lengths to help and keep her safe – even when it brings him into conflict with his friends, most notably Lucas.

This loyalty to those he cares about continues to show itself in the second season: refusing to believe that El is dead, he calls her every night using his Supercom, and continuing to show concern for Will when it becomes clear that his friend's stay in the Upside Down has left its sinister mark.

Still, as always, everything comes back to Dungeons & Dragons. Mike is a born dungeon master, and it's his and his friends' realisation of the Upside Down's monster's similarity to the game's Mind Flayer that informs their tactics on how to stop it.

Best of all, El returns to help save the day, leading to an emotional reunion with Mike. The day saved, there's even time for them to share a tender moment during their first dance at the Snow Ball.

The following year, the two are fully in the throes of teenage passion – despite the increasingly futile attempts of El's new guardian, Hopper, to get between the two. Sure, there are hitches – they briefly break up after Hopper tells Mike to stay away from her, after which El uses her power to spy on Mike – but it's fairly standard for young love.

Regardless, soon enough the Mind Flayer is back, and it's Mike's turn to save El for a change, clubbing a possessed Billy with a baseball bat in the process, before witnessing the big confrontation that sees the Mind Flayer apparently destroyed once and for all.

However, the ending is bittersweet. With Hopper apparently dead, El is forced to leave Hawkins with the Byers family. It may be goodbye, but not forever, as they promise to see each other soon.

Exactly what the future holds for Mike and El remains unknown, judging by what we saw in season four. Mike was by El's side as she tried to ensure their friends in Hawkins survived Vecna's attack, and his support helped her gain control, but their lives are still in danger.

Whatever happens in Hawkins and beyond in future episodes, judging by what we've seen of the series so far, you can expect Mike to be a central part of proceedings.

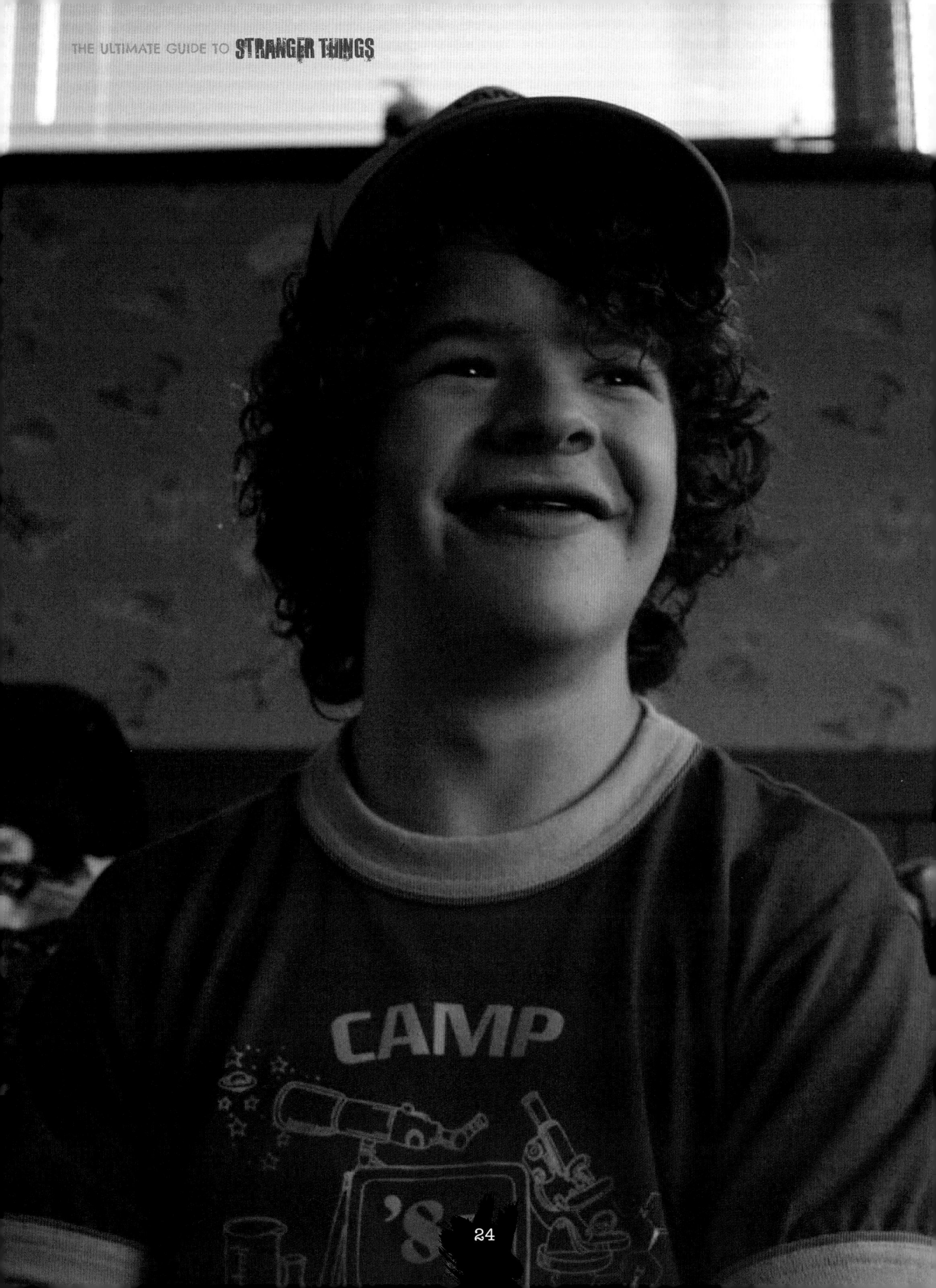
CAMP

DUSTIN HENDERSON

THE BEATING HEART OF THE GROUP IS
UTTERLY LOVEABLE IN EVERY WAY

The beating heart and gentle soul of the group, Dustin (Gaten Matarazzo) is many people's favourite character in the show, and for good reason. He's a peacemaker, full of determination, and possesses an underrated ability to bring out the best in people.

Like his best friends, Mike Wheeler, Lucas Sinclair and Will Byers, Dustin is a Dungeons & Dragons devotee and committed member of the school's AV club. It's these interests that play a pivotal role in uncovering the mystery when Will goes missing.

Throughout the saga of Will's disappearance and the subsequent arrival into their lives of Eleven, Dustin plays a proactive role, getting vital information from their teacher, Mr Clarke, and making sure that Mike and Lucas reconcile after El saves them from some bullies. During this first season, he proves to be the glue in the group, keeping them on track right until Will is rescued.

The following year, Dustin has two things on his mind: games and girls. More specifically, who keeps beating their high scores at Palace Arcade? New arrival Max Mayfield proves to be the answer to both questions.

While he initially battles Lucas for her affections, his true love this season is Dart, a miniature Demogorgon he unwittingly befriends. Turns out he'll forgive him anything, even eating the family cat, Mews.

A slightly more fruitful relationship is the one he develops with a certain Steve Harrington. Having enlisted Steve's help against the Demogorgons, Steve becomes something of a father figure to Dustin, something he's clearly missing. Steve offers advice on girls, the secret of how to have incredible hair, and even drops him off outside the Snow Ball.

While the end-of-year finale is unsuccessful on the girlfriend front for Dustin, his spirits are lifted by Nancy Wheeler, who cheers him up by offering him the slow dance his peers had denied him, in one of the show's most heartwarming moments.

As it turns out, Dustin doesn't have to wait too long for some romance, meeting a girl named Suzie at Camp Know Where, with Dustin even building a ham radio device (named 'Cerebro', naturally) in order to make sure the two stay in touch.

Not that any of his friends really believe him – indeed, it's a strange time for Dustin. With Mike and Lucas paired up with El and Max, Dustin ends up spending most of his time with Steve and Robin at the Starcourt Mall when he unintentionally intercepts a Russian transmission on Cerebro.

After discovering another gate below the mall, he and his friends once again team up to defeat the Mind Flayer – his and Suzie's rendition of 'Neverending Story' over Cerebro providing the utterly awesome centrepiece.

With Will and El having departed, and Dustin's gang having gifted their beloved D&D set to Lucas's younger sister Erica, it will be all change for Dustin and co going forward. But, as long as he continues to hang out with Steve, regale us with fascinating facts and save the day in awesome fashion, we'll be happy.

LUCAS SINCLAIR

AS THE DUNGEON AND WEAPONS MASTER, LUCAS IS THE LEVEL-HEADED TACTICIAN OF THE GROUP

A core member of the gang at the heart of *Stranger Things*, Lucas (Caleb McLaughlin) is best friends with Will Byers, Dustin Henderson and Mike Wheeler, sharing a love of all things geeky, especially Dungeons & Dragons.

When Will goes missing and the group first encounter Eleven, we get a bit more of an idea of the dynamic of the group: while Mike and Dustin are more believing of her, Lucas is the sceptical one. This outlook isn't helped when it turns out that El is deliberately keeping them from the Upside Down (understandably, in fairness), but Lucas isn't happy. He's even less happy when she telekinetically hurls him after he gets in a fight with Mike.

Still, as tends to happen after kids fight, they quickly make up, but not before Lucas successfully warns the gang of trouble afoot. Later on, he joins the group as they help El defeat the Demogorgon at the school, before reuniting with the rescued Will in hospital.

A year later, and it's love in the air. Determined to find out who keeps beating his top score on *Dragon's Lair* at the Palace Arcade, he later finds out it's newly arrived redhead Max Mayfield. Unfortunately, she also has an absolutely terrifying older step-brother, Billy Hargrove, who isn't averse to casually attempting to run them off the road.

Regardless, this doesn't put Lucas or Dustin off vying for Max's affections, accepting her into the group and inviting her to join in with their adventures, even while they have bigger fish to fry, what with looking after mini Demogorgon 'Dart', and trying to work out what's up with Will again.

Ultimately, it's Lucas who wins this particular battle, kissing Max at the Snow Ball in the season two finale. A year later, and they're still together, bickering like a regular married couple beyond their tender years and, more often than not, hanging out at Starcourt Mall.

In the group, Lucas seems to take on the role of an elder statesman of sorts, dishing out relationship advice to a grateful Mike (even though it's not always good advice), and helping out as Hawkins comes under assault yet again from the fearsome creatures that inhabit the Upside Down.

Yet he's far more than just the level-headed one; he's a born tactician and natural leader, helming the boys' Dungeons & Dragons sessions, adept at using a slingshot, and not afraid to stand up to bullies – or in the case of Billy, absolutely terrifying older brothers.

He also shows real signs of coming of age, accepting El into the group despite his initial misgivings, later forgiving her for spying on him and Mike, asking for advice when it's needed (like when he asked his dad about how to apologise to girls), and gifting their beloved D&D set to his irritating younger sister Erica.

Always a sceptic, as long as he remains the voice of reason the gang needs, we'll let him off.

27

WILL BYERS

THIS POOR BOY HAS ENDURED MORE THAN PEOPLE TRIPLE HIS AGE, BUT HIS ROCK-SOLID RESOLVE NEVER WAVERS

A quiet kid living in the tranquil woodland outskirts of Hawkins, the life of Will Byers (Noah Schnapp) turned quite literally upside down when he was abducted by an otherworldly creature on 6 November 1983. Before the ordeal, Will was a sweet lad who enjoyed playing Dungeons & Dragons with his friends Mike, Dustin and Lucas, and enjoyed the company of his mother Joyce and older brother Jonathan. He was well-liked by those he loved, and for a good reason: Will Byers could do no wrong; he was the perfect kid.

The strong bonds he formed proved pivotal when he went missing, as his friends and family bent over backwards to bring him home. Kidnapped by a Demogorgon and held captive in the Upside Down, we don't actually see much of him in the first season. Rather, we learn about him through his friends and family. Known as 'Will The Wise' to his D&D 'party', we aptly discover that Will uses his wisdom to his advantage – demonstrated when he learns to communicate with his mother across worlds using fairy lights.

Through the efforts of Sheriff Hopper and his mother Joyce, Will is rescued from the Upside Down. However, his harrowing ordeal is never far from his mind. Will feels coddled by his friends and family, he's called 'Zombie Boy' at school, and he soon learns that something much more malevolent than the Demogorgon has plans for him. Will has been possessed by the Mind Flayer, an otherworldly creature from the Upside Down. As he tries to readjust to his life, he is plagued by glimpses of the gargantuan beast looming over Hawkins.

The Mind Flayer's hold over Will becomes so powerful it is able to speak through and control him. With the help of Jonathan, Joyce and Nancy, it is exorcised from Will's body, severing his connection to the Upside Down.

Will is more than happy to immerse himself in the worlds of D&D, comics and *The Lord of the Rings* – his reluctance to 'grow up' could be a lasting effect of the trauma he endured during the Upside Down. This part of him causes a schism with his friends during the summer of 1985. Dustin, Mike and Lucas are too concerned with chasing girls, where Will just wants to cast himself as Dungeon Master and play adventure.

A second incursion from the Mind Flayer brings the party back together once again, however, and Will uses his latent 'second sight' ability to sense the monster's presence. He also takes part in the fight against the Spider Monster in the Starcourt Mall by throwing fireworks at their foe.

After leaving Hawkins and reuniting with Mike in California, Will tracks down the location of the Nina Project and heads there to warn that Eleven's life is in danger. Worryingly, he has a feeling that Vecna is regaining his strength ready to strike again.

JOYCE BYERS

MEET THE MOTHER WHO WOULDN'T GIVE UP ON HER CHILD

The story of Joyce Byers (Winona Ryder) in *Stranger Things* begins with every mother's worst nightmare being realised: her child going missing. It's this abduction that drives the plot, but it's ultimately Joyce's refusal to give up on her son that saves the day.

A dedicated mother to Jonathan and Will, Joyce has pretty much been left to man Fort Byers alone after the departure of her feckless ex-husband, Lonnie, so it would be understandable if she has a bit of a breakdown, as everyone assumes she has when she plasters the walls of her house with letters.

However, that's not true. Realising that Will is trapped somewhere and attempting to communicate with her, she provides him with a means to do so. Even when his 'body' is discovered in the nearby quarry, she refuses to believe he's dead. Eventually getting former schoolfriend Hopper onside, she teams up with Eleven and her sons' friends, and ventures into the Upside Down to rescue Will. Celebrating a while later with Christmas dinner, it appears to be a case of happily ever after.

However, it's not to be. While everyone seems to have moved on, with Joyce shacking up with another former schoolfriend (not that she was aware of him), 'Superhero' Bob Newby, everything's not okay with Will.

Eventually, Joyce cottons on, and it becomes clear that Will is still experiencing visions of the Upside Down. When things take a turn for the worse, she takes him to Hawkins Lab. When it gets overrun by Demodogs, she is only just able to escape – Bob, however, isn't so lucky.

Despite this devastating blow, Joyce is able to help exorcise the Mind Flayer from Will's body. So it's a bittersweet ending for Joyce – her son is safe, but she's lost someone she had real feelings for.

He isn't the only one, though. While her and Hopper have grown closer, she's understandably reluctant to commit, considering everything she's been through. Regardless, there isn't much time to dwell, as there are more mysterious goings-on in Hawkins. The discovery of a hidden Russian base is inevitably connected to the Upside Down, and into another adventure they're pulled.

The chemistry between Joyce and Hopper continues to grow to the point where it seems like she might finally be acknowledging Murray's advice to "tear off those clothes and get it over with already", promising a dinner date with Hopper once it's all over.

Sadly, they never get the chance. With Hopper forced to stay behind in order to close the gate, he seemingly sacrifices himself to do so, leaving Joyce devastated once more.

As far as Hawkins is concerned, this is the final straw. Following through on her earlier plans, Joyce departs to Lenora Hills in California alongside her sons and Eleven.

Just as she seems to be settling into a life of normality, Joyce discovers that Hopper might still be alive and goes off to track him down.

JIM HOPPER

IRRESPONSIBLE? MAYBE. VIOLENT? POSSIBLY. HEROIC? CERTAINLY. POLICE CHIEF JIM HOPPER IS ABSOLUTELY HAWKINS' NUMBER-ONE LAWMAN

The chief of police in the sleepy town of Hawkins, we first encounter Jim Hopper (David Harbour) as he is carrying decades' worth of demons on his back. An alcoholic, apathetic chain smoker, the premature death of his daughter and collapse of his marriage sent the lawman on a downward spiral that he struggles to escape. The mundane life in Hawkins doesn't help; he can get away with oversleeping and abusing pills and the bottle… that is, until the curious case of Will Byers falls onto his desk.

Will's suspicious abduction stirs a dormant dynamism in Hopper, making him spring into action to bring Joyce Byers' son home. It turns out that deep down, buried under the pill packets, empty beer cans and cigarette cartons, Hopper is the hero Hawkins needs. Capable, brave and compassionate, Hopper's laser-focused drive to solve the mystery of Will's disappearance leads him down a rabbit hole of conspiracy and the supernatural – all of which has been happening under his nose. Confounding the case even further is the sudden appearance of a child who only goes by the name Eleven.

Hopper's brash fist-first gumshoe approach to the mystery might not be conventional, but it gets results. After discovering Will's whereabouts thanks to a brush with Hawkins Lab, Hopper and Joyce travel to the Upside Down and rescue the young boy. With his mission complete, Hopper finds purpose in life and chooses to take Eleven in, sheltering her from the shady scientists hunting her.

Hopper and Eleven build a warm relationship, allowing the Chief's past wounds to heal and giving her the father she deserves. However, Hopper's over-protectiveness pushes Eleven away as she becomes frustrated with their isolation in a remote forest cabin. Meanwhile, the Upside Down's hold on Hawkins strengthens, and Hopper discovers a network of tunnels below the town that again puts him at odds with the scientists at Hawkins Lab.

After a confrontation with Mike Wheeler, Hopper realises he is too coddling of Eleven and reconciles with her – and just in time, too. He escorts his daughter below Hawkins to a gateway under Hawkins Lab to the Upside Down, where she seals the portal. With a forged birth certificate in hand for 'Jane Hopper', Jim loosens his grip on his adopted daughter and lets her experience the life of a teenage girl.

In 1985, sporting a *Magnum PI*-style 'stache-and-shirt combo, things kick off yet again. Hopper and Joyce embark on another fistfight-laden quest as they discover Russian agents working under the town.

This time, however, Hopper's headstrong attitude gets the better of him, and he finds himself on the wrong side of a closing portal, cutting him off from his loved ones in a heroic moment of self-sacrifice. In his final moments, we see him smiling reassuringly to a distraught Joyce, demonstrating his bravery in the face of danger.

Hopper's story is far from over, though. In fact, it has taken an odd, some might say 'strange' turn, as he's revealed to be toiling away in a Russian labour camp thousands of miles from Hawkins. How is Hopp going to get out of this one?

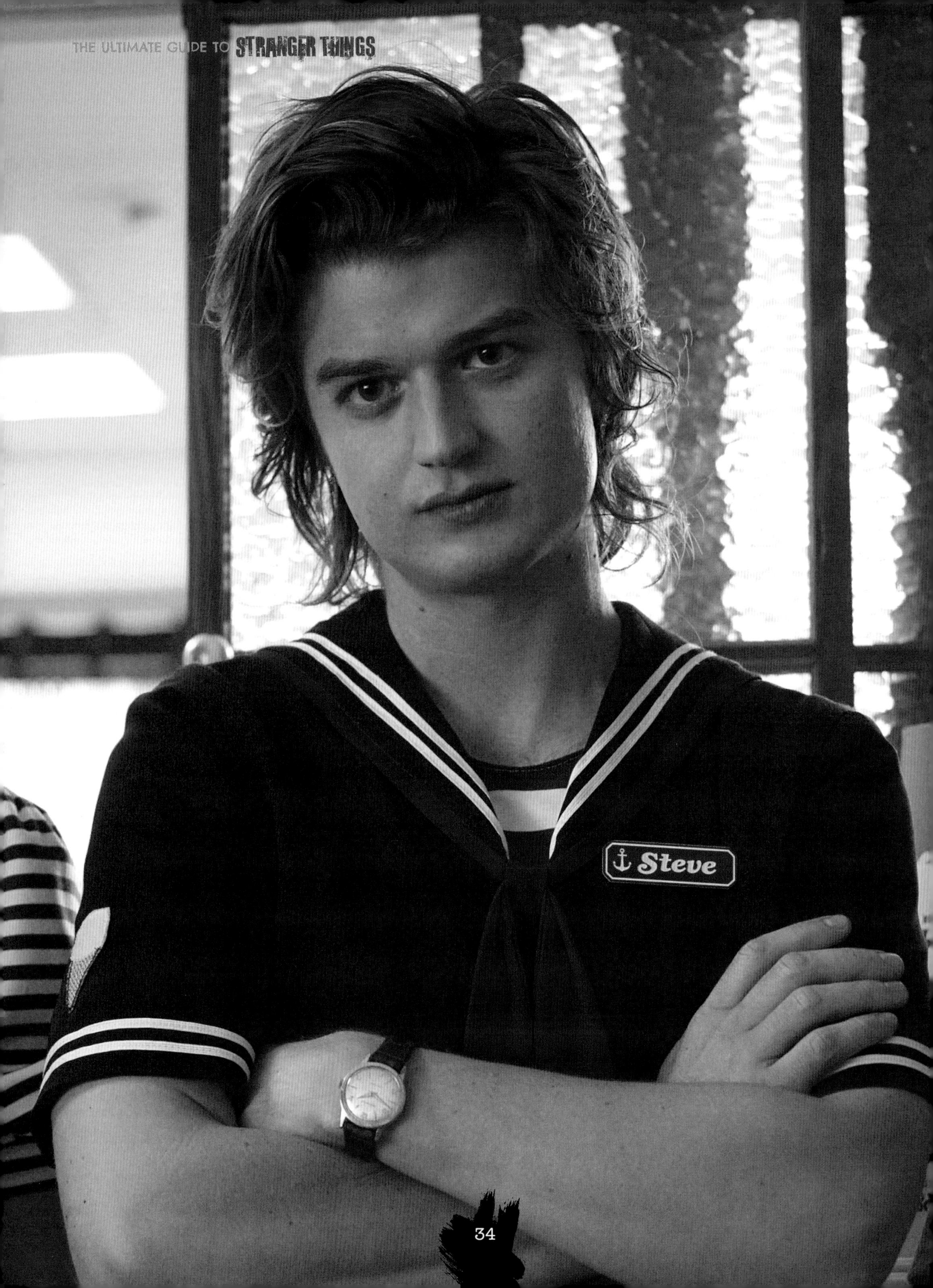
Steve

STEVE HARRINGTON

FROM HIGH SCHOOL ZERO TO BRAVE-HEARTED HERO, STEVE'S STORY IS ONE FOR HAWKINS HISTORIANS

We first meet Steve Harrington (Joe Keery) as the boyfriend of Nancy Wheeler. A stereotypical popular high-school kid, the attitude of 'King Steve' leaves a lot to be desired, with him being mean, vapid and romantically pushy. However, throughout the series, we see him evolve into a full-on hero with a heart of gold who frequently takes one for the team.

In the first season, Steve is a reluctant antagonist. His insecurities often put him at odds with Nancy and high-school outcast Jonathan Byers. In an effort to maintain his stratospheric popularity with his peer-pressuring 'popular kid' crew, Steve talks down to and bullies those he considers beneath him. In one scene, Steve cruelly destroys Jonathan's beloved camera.

Yet, after dining on some humble pie when Nancy leaves him, Steve rises to the mantle of hero when he helps Jonathan and Nancy defend the Byers' house from a Demogorgon. Spiked bat in hand, he battles the creature, giving Jonathan a chance to set the beast ablaze. Afterwards, Steve reconciles with Nancy and even buys Jonathan a replacement camera, fully solidifying him as one of the good guys.

During the Mind Flayer crisis of 1984, Steve's personal life takes a nosedive. His school popularity is overthrown by Hawkins newcomer and all-around bad boy Billy Hargrove, and his relationship with Nancy fizzles out.

Steve finds a new purpose by bonding with Dustin Henderson. When the curly-haired kid enlists Steve to help 'deal' with his pet Demogorgon, Dart, our hero once again takes up his spiked baseball bat and makes a stand in a junkyard to defend Dustin's friends from a horde of Demo-dogs. Steve builds a rapport with the kids, especially Dustin, who he takes under his wing. This newfound parental instinct kicks into overdrive when he has to face down and subsequently take a pounding from his high-school nemesis, Billy, to protect his new pre-teen pals.

Steve finishes the second season battered and down on his luck, but not alone. He finds a friend and surrogate little brother in Dustin, and graduates high school – only to find himself with poor grades, few prospects and selling ice-cream at Scoops Ahoy.

Dressed in a sailor uniform and forced to endure a frosty working relationship with fellow Scoops Ahoy worker Robin Buckley, Steve suffers humiliation working at the Starcourt Mall in summer 1985.

But this is Hawkins, and there's always *something* lurking around the corner. In Steve's case, it's Russian spies. Teaming up with Robin, Dustin and Lucas Sinclair's sister Erica, Steve helps uncover a red scare right under the mall. In the process, he takes another knuckle sandwich to the face from a Russian brute during an interrogation session, but finds a kindred spirit in Robin, and ends up taking up a better job with her at Hawkins Family Video.

It always seems to be a 'you lose some, you win some' situation with Steve, and that's perhaps why we like him so much. Following his redemption arc in season one, he has managed to turn a bad situation on its head multiple times. Always charismatic, and with a rocking Eighties haircut to boot, there's no way you can't be drawn to King Steve.

NANCY WHEELER

WHETHER SHE'S ARMED WITH A BASEBALL BAT, FIREWORKS OR A TAPE RECORDER, YOU WOULDN'T WANT TO BET AGAINST NANCY WHEELER

Perhaps more than anyone else in the series – apart from Steve Harrington – Nancy Wheeler (Natalia Dyer) presents the best example of *Stranger Things*' ability to take first impressions of a character and quickly turn them on their head.

Initially presented as Mike's intelligent yet easily led elder sister, Nancy has evolved over the course of the show to arguably become its moral centre: unwilling to let things go when just about everyone else has given up. It's a bit of a journey to get to this point, though. Not that she's a bad person; she just does what a lot of teenagers do: ignore her parents, argue with her younger brother and lie about where she's going in order to hook up with the boy she likes.

However, in the world of *Stranger Things*, mistakes seem to be punished that bit more harshly, as we see with the fate of Nancy's best friend Barb. Having been cast aside at a poolhouse meet-up, Nancy is occupied while her best friend is taken and ultimately killed by the Demogorgon.

Finally coming to her senses, she teams up with Jonathan to investigate Barb's disappearance, playing a vital role in locating the Demogorgon – and Will Byers, in the process – although this confirms the death of Barb.

Guilt-ridden, Nancy breaks up with Steve, later teaming up with Jonathan once more while they attempt to trick Dr Owens at the lab into disclosing the truth of what happened to Barb. Successfully done, they once again help save the day, assisting Joyce in restraining Will as the Mind Flayer is exorcised from his body.

Season three begins on a high for Nancy – she's together with Jonathan, justice for Barb has been achieved, and she's even cheered up Dustin by dancing with him at the Snow Ball.

However, her positivity is brought crashing down by her experiences as an intern at the *Hawkins Post*. Jeered at by her misogynistic male colleagues, it's only a timely pep talk from her mother, Karen, that gets her back on her feet.

What results is a catharsis of sorts, as while continuing with their investigation, Nancy and Jonathan face off against mind-flayed versions of their horrible former co-workers, ultimately defeating them.

Nancy again plays a vital role in the battle at Starcourt Mall, lobbing fireworks at the Mind Flayer to help cover Eleven's escape.

However, it's ultimately a bittersweet ending. With Hopper presumed dead following the lab explosion, Joyce decides to finally up sticks and leave Hawkins, taking Eleven, Will and Jonathan with her. Granted, it's not the saddest moment in an episode peppered with sad moments, but it's still gutting to see the young lovers separated.

Trying to take her mind off Jonathan, Nancy gets involved in the Hawkins murders and finds out about Vecna, consequently becoming one of his potential victims.

KAREN WHEELER

THE WHEELER FAMILY MATRIARCH BALANCES HER CHALLENGING FAMILY WITH HER YEARNING FOR SOME EXCITEMENT IN HER OWN LIFE

Wife to Ted, and mother to Nancy, Mike and Holly, Karen Wheeler (Cara Buono) dotes on her family – not that she gets much appreciation for it. When the series starts, Nancy is often off with her new friends, and Mike is preoccupied with looking for Will and hiding Eleven, leaving Karen to man fort Wheeler with little Holly on her hip.

With the borderline oblivious Ted largely leaving the parental duties to Karen, she has to do the bulk of the parenting groundwork, making her seem overbearing as a result. For the most part, her pleas for them to talk to her fall on deaf ears.

Having married Ted young, the flames of passion have died out in their marriage long ago, which makes it understandable – if ill-advised – when Karen reacts

positively to the flirtings of Billy Hargrove when he comes knocking for his sister.

Having invested in a new hairdo – and swimsuit – she successfully catches his eye at the local swimming pool once more, and arranges a secret rendezvous. However, at the last moment her conscience gets the better of her, and she backs out. This is probably just as well, since Billy has been possessed by the Mind Flayer by this point.

Despite almost making a bad decision, she's there for her children when they need her the most, giving Nancy a timely pep talk after her firing from the *Hawkins Post*, and comforting Mike when Will and El leave Hawkins.

So, in summary: not perfect by any means, but a good mother when it matters.

JONATHAN BYERS

"DO YOU WANNA BE NORMAL? DO YOU WANNA BE JUST LIKE EVERYONE ELSE? BEING A FREAK IS THE BEST. I'M A FREAK!"

When Will's older brother arrives home late from work in the first season's pilot, he couldn't imagine the repercussions his extended shift would have. As Will is catapulted into the Upside Down, the crisis brings intelligent, introverted Jonathan (Charlie Heaton) out of his shell.

Season one sees him step up as a big brother when Will is missing, uncharacteristically challenge Steve Harrington to a fist-fight, stand up to his abusive father Lonnie and ultimately face off with the monsters of the Upside Down. Jonathan's a keen photographer, perceptively commenting that, "Sometimes people don't really say what they're thinking. But you capture the right moment... it says more." He is passionate about music, introducing Will to The Clash and compiling a mixtape with the likes of David Bowie and Joy Division.

Where he excels in the arts, however, he's less capable when it comes to social interactions, preferring solitude. Jonathan might be shy, but he's brave, loyal and comfortable being an outsider; he follows his own path with deep introspection, encouraging Will to do the same. While he might show a general disdain for other people, he is devoted to those he loves, particularly his younger brother, even if he can sometimes find it hard to open up to them. Jonathan shows his kindness and compassion through actions rather than words. Now in California, and despite his antisocial nature, Jonathan has finally made a non-familiar new best friend in the form of stoner and pizza delivery guy Argyle.

DR MARTIN BRENNER

PAPA'S RUTHLESSLY AMBITIOUS APPROACH TO SCIENCE IS RESPONSIBLE FOR ALL THE CHAOS INFLICTED UPON HAWKINS

The closest thing El had to a father figure before Hopper, Martin Brenner (Matthew Modine) is a brilliant yet psychopathic scientist. He is a native of Hawkins, attending high school in the town before becoming involved in the CIA-sanctioned Project MKUltra. As director of Hawkins National Laboratory he began experimenting on college students – one of whom was Terry Ives – in order to develop mind-control techniques.

After discovering that Terry was pregnant he stole her baby, Jane, and raised her in the lab, giving her the number 011 and studying the psychokinetic abilities she developed due to the experiments he had subjected her mother to. He displays highly manipulative traits and very little empathy or consideration for others. As Papa, he would regularly put El through cruel psychological torture, despite her being a child, and never gave her any love or socialisation.

Brenner is also responsible for the gate into the Upside Down opening, releasing the monstrous creatures and toxic biological matter, as he encouraged El to make contact with the Demogorgon when spying on a Russian agent in the void. He is unscrupulous and shows a total disregard for human life. In an attempt to cover up the repercussions of his work, he faked Will Byers' death and is keen to let the chaos continue in Hawkins as long as it advances his scientific understanding. It's suggested that he may have survived the attack of the Demogorgon in season one's finale, but even in his absence from seasons two and three his memory continues to haunt El, while his actions have a never-ending impact on Hawkins. In season four, he is revealed to have survived and to be working with Dr Owens on a new secret initiative, the Nina Project, designed to rejuvenate Eleven's lost psychokinetic powers.

MAXINE 'MAX' MAYFIELD

A VIDEOGAME VIRTUOSO, STAR SKATER AND FIERCE FRIEND, MAX WILL ALWAYS HAVE YOUR BACK

In October 1984, the local arcade hummed with excitement as a newcomer smashed high-score records on the videogame machines. Their calling card? The name MADMAX proudly displayed at the top of the high-score screen.

This was the alias used by Maxine Mayfield (Sadie Sink), who had moved from California to Hawkins, Indiana, with her mother, stepfather and rage-filled stepbrother, Billy Hargrove. Her impressive gaming skills drew the attention of Dustin and Lucas, who invited her to join their 'Party'. While Max's relationship with the group was unsteady at first, she soon demonstrated her worth to the crew by helping them hunt down Dustin's pet Demogorgon, Dart, and later saved Steve Harrington from a near-fatal beating from Billy by stabbing her stepbrother with a sedative.

Skilled with a skateboard, lockpick and behind the wheel of a car, Max is the natural rogue (or "zoomer", in her own words) of the Party. She is fiercely protective of her friends – in particular, she keeps Eleven close and helps introduce her to the life of a teenager. She also has a soft spot for Lucas and struck up a romantic relationship with him after they kissed at the Snow Ball – the pair have been lovebirds ever since.

Despite their fraught relationship, and after all the hurt he caused, Max loved her stepbrother and we see her mourning him months after he died saving the Party from the Spider Monster at the Starcourt Mall. Max is then dramatically involved with Vecna as the pair try to kill each other – this is undoubtedly 'her season'. Her series-stealing scenes in season four are scored with the 1980s Kate Bush track Running Up That Hill – which leapt to the top of the charts on the back of the show.

BILLY HARGROVE

THE GANG'S FORMER TORMENTOR BECOMES SEASON 3'S MAIN ANTAGONIST, ONLY TO TRAGICALLY REDEEM HIMSELF

ntroduced in *Stranger Things'* second season, Billy Hargrove (Dacre Montgomery) moves to Hawkins with his step-sister Max Mayfield. Billy is a bully, attempting to control and intimidate Max, as well as her friends and anyone else who happens to get in his way.

Pulling up to school in a blue Camaro and striking up a rivalry with Steve Harrington, his bad boy persona and fit physique gets him noticed by the ladies, particularly when he works as a lifeguard at Hawkins Community Pool in season three, but he displays a misogynistic attitude, hooking up with a new girl everyday, arrogantly attempting to start an affair with Mrs Wheeler and commenting to Steve that "there are always other bitches" when his relationship with Nancy is on the rocks.

At times, however, Billy shows glimpses of care and a protective instinct towards his step-sister Max, even if his way of showing it comes over as toxic and controlling.

When the Mind Flayer implants part of itself in Billy's brain in season three he accrues an army of followers, who are all possessed by the Flayer in its attempt to annihilate everyone. When El accesses Billy's memories, we witness his last true moment of happiness – surfing with his mother. Before she left due to his father's abuse, he was a happy and friendly boy, and it is revealed that he only became a bully when the violence his dad inflicted upon her was transferred onto him. It is the happy memory of his mother that El uses to reignite the humanity in Billy, and he ultimately sacrifices himself to save the gang, gasping "I'm sorry" to Max before taking his last breath.

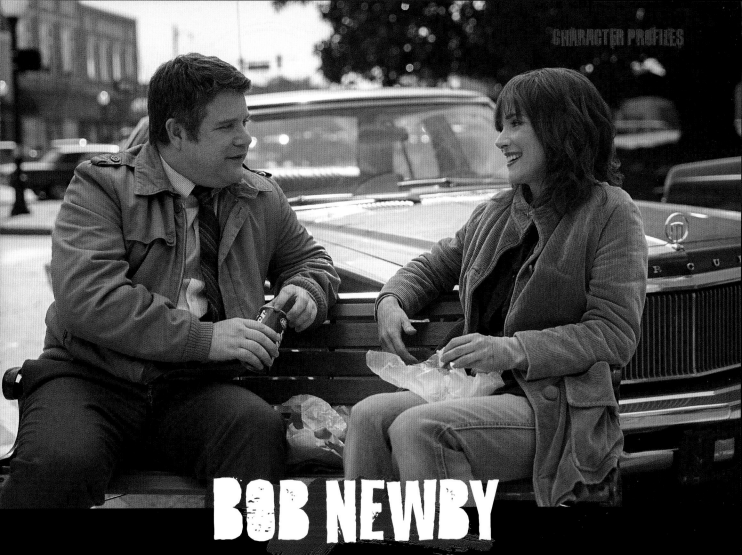

BOB NEWBY

HIS STAY ON THE SHOW WAS SHORT-LIVED, BUT NO ONE WILL EVER FORGET BOB NEWBY SUPERHERO

Also known as 'Bob Newby Superhero', Bob (Sean Astin) is one of those rare examples of a person who genuinely is what they seem: an authentic and wholehearted individual who will go out of his way to help others.

A former classmate of Jim Hopper and Joyce Byers, he ends up dating the latter in season two. He was also the founder of the Hawkins Middle AV Club that the boys participate in. Basically, it's thanks to his early efforts that they were able to save Will!

As well as being a devoted boyfriend to Joyce, he does his best to be there for Will, always being on hand for advice (even if some of this is questionable – turns out the Mind

Flayer doesn't take kindly to being told to "Go away").

The way events transpire, Bob plays a key role in the events of the second season, working out where Hopper is trapped by deciphering Will's drawings, and drawing on his knowledge of BASIC to turn the power in the lab back on and rescue everyone. Sadly, his heroic actions come at the cost of his own life, as his escape from the facility is foiled by a group of Demodogs. Such a beloved character really did not deserve to die in such a gruesome way.

So while Bob is no more, he lives on both in our hearts, and on Will's 'Bob Newby Superhero' drawing that he affixes to the Byers family refrigerator.

DR SAM OWENS

WHEN IT'S GAME OVER FOR DR BRENNER, UP STEPS DR OWENS

The successor to the nefarious Dr Brenner as Director of Operations at Hawkins Lab, Dr Sam Owens (Paul Reiser) isn't the outright villain his predecessor was.

Sure, he's determined to keep the Upside Down a secret, and he isn't averse to working for a shady government agency with a vaguely defined purpose, but he has perfectly legitimate reasons for keeping the Upside Down under wraps – namely, what would happen if certain governments had access to it.

He's also a hell of a lot nicer to his patients – while Brenner put Eleven through hell, he's a lot more careful with Will (although he's not averse to putting him through the odd telepathic burning session).

Regardless, he shows by his actions that he's not completely in it for himself, first by risking death in order to make sure that Joyce and Hopper make it out the lab safely when they're threatened by the Demodogs.

His finest moment, however, comes when he provides Eleven with a forged birth certificate cementing her status as Hopper's daughter. He may not have really had any involvement in her mistreatment, but it's nice to see someone attempting to make amends.

He turns up with the US military after the incident with the Gate at Starcourt Mall, too late to have any impact on the situation. But during a limited but important appearance in season four, he then does something very useful in helping Eleven to get her powers back.

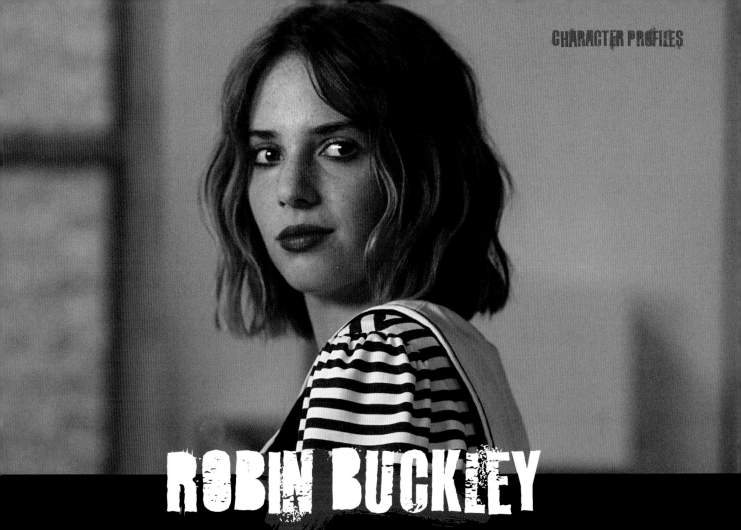

ROBIN BUCKLEY

THE SCOOPS AHOY EMPLOYEE COVERS HER TRUE FEELINGS WITH A VENEER OF SARCASM

First arriving on the show as Steve Harrington's co-worker at Scoops Ahoy, Robin (Maya Hawke) has a history with the one she refers to as 'Dingus' that he is completely oblivious to.

At first, she couldn't appear anymore different to him; he's all about his reputation and reliving past glories, while with Robin – according to her – having no reputation to speak of, she's far more at ease with saying and doing whatever she wants.

Initially taking pleasure in mocking Steve during their working hours, she eventually gets drawn into his and Dustin's investigation into the source of the Russian transmissions, with her language skills proving to be a vital asset in decoding what is being said.

While she's arguably a bit irresponsible (along with Steve, of course) in allowing Dustin and Erica to get caught up in what is in reality an extremely dangerous situation, she shows bravery in facing up to the menacing Russian agents. All the while, it's clear that her mockery of Steve and frequent sarcasm is overcompensating for something.

Facing interrogation and truth serum, Robin and Steve finally reveal their deepest secrets to each other. Steve loves Robin, and Robin loves... another girl. Despite Steve's surprise, he's completely accepting of Robin's revelation, and her coming out only serves to deepen their bond.

Robin goes on to team up with Nancy to uncover the secrets of the Creel family and has her own close call with Vecna

ERICA SINCLAIR

THERE'S MORE TO HER THAN JUST ANNOYING HER OLDER BROTHER

The stereotypical annoying younger sister, Erica (Priah Ferguson) likes nothing more than showing her brother Lucas as much disrespect as possible. Whether it be using his stuff without permission or calling him a nerd, she delights in giving him a hard time.

Laughing at his *Ghostbusters* costume? Check. Listening in on his radio chat? Check. Mocking his prom outfit and practice asking-out attempts? Check, check and check.

By the events of season three, she's still annoying her brother, although she prefers to spend most of her time with her friends at the new Starcourt Mall.

This time, however, she takes on a more important role in proceedings, assisting Steve, Dustin and Robin in their attempts to uncover the mystery of what's going on in the mall. Her actions are far from selfless, however; she just wants some free ice cream.

In the process, she shows that she's not all mouth: when faced with the possibility of death at the hands of Russian agents, she's more annoyed at the prospect of missing out on a sleepover.

For all her mocking of Lucas and his friends, however, she has serious nerd credentials herself: her *My Little Pony* knowledge is second to none. Plus, she's not exactly displeased at being left the gang's old Dungeons & Dragons sets, hinting at a future as geeky as her brother's. She'd deny any similarities with him whatsoever though, obviously. That would be so lame.

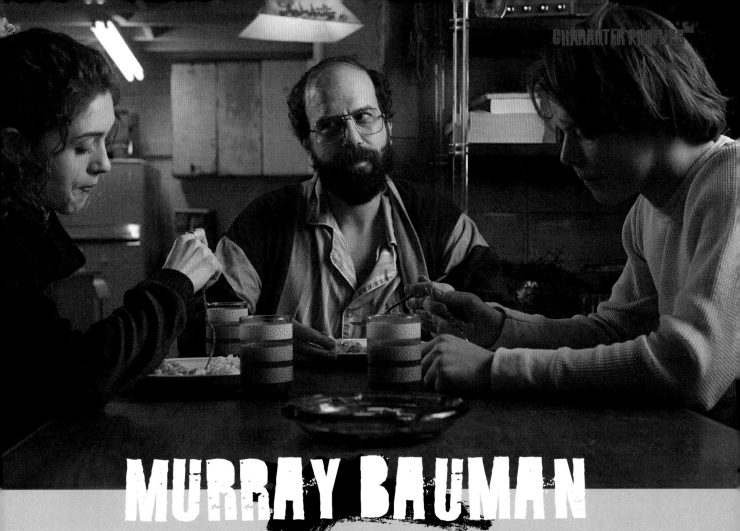

MURRAY BAUMAN

STRANGER THINGS' UNOFFICIAL LOVE DOCTOR IS ALSO THE SHOW'S UNSPOKEN HERO

A former investigative journalist, when we first meet him, Murray Bauman (Brett Gelman) is working as a private investigator, having been hired by Barb's parents to look into their daughter's mysterious disappearance.

Living in a run-down shack in Illinois, Murray isn't taken seriously by most due to his eccentricity and lack of regard for dress, personal hygiene or social niceties, but this demeanour hides a shrewd and sharp individual with a strong sense of duty.

For a start, he seems to be spot-on about almost anything. He predicts the Russian spy presence in Hawkins a long time before anyone else notices, and exasperatedly points out when couples are a match even before they themselves are fully aware of it – first with Nancy and Jonathan, and then again with Joyce and Hopper.

Having been given the brush-off by Hopper after confiding in him his suspicions of some weird goings-on (partially because he was correct in his suspicions), he later gives Nancy and Jonathan some advice in order to help get the lab shut down – a success he's later to bask in.

A year later, he's back helping out Hopper and Joyce in interrogating Russian prisoner Alexei – who despite his suspicions regarding his country of birth, he later bonds with – before accompanying the trio to the fair and later the mall, in their attempts to get the portal shut down. He then accompanies Joyce to Alaska to help Joyce spring Hopper from prison. Yep, it's fair to say that Bauman is the unsung hero of the show.

EDDIE MUNSON

THE MISUNDERSTOOD METALHEAD IS CENTRAL TO THE ACTION OF SEASON FOUR AND SIMPLY MASTERFUL IN THE FINALE

Season four newcomer Eddie Munson (Joseph Quinn) became a huge fan-favourite as the leader of the Dungeons and Dragons Hellfire Club at Hawkins High – the new school where we find Dustin, Mike and Lucas in episode one.

Charismatic Eddie is still rocking around the place with his band Corroded Coffin a full two years after he should have graduated, having not yet made the grades.

He comes to play a pivotal role in the story, at the centre of a murder investigation when cheerleader Chrissy is found dead at his home and he goes on the run.

For such a new character it's incredible how quickly he makes his presence felt – it seems like he's been around for ever. Considering that he spends a lot of time in hiding, cast out by the town in echoes of the 'satanic panic' which took a hold in 1980s North America, Eddie's impact is truly phenomenal. From his early scenes making friends with Dustin and the gang and picking up with Chrissy; through to his epic guitar scene in the final battle to defeat Vecna, where he becomes the selfless hero of the hour, Eddie is never less than super-impressive. His one-man rendition of Master of Puppets by Metallica, which he rocks out to distract Vecna's Demobats is superb and rivals the season's Running Up That Hill motif for the 'most memorable musical moment' award.

His untimely death left Dustin sobbing, and viewers believed that the character deserved better. He never even got to meet Eleven!

JASON CARVER

THE GOLDEN BOY OF HAWKINS HIGH USES HIS POWERS OF PERSUASION TO STIR UP MORE TROUBLE IN HAWKINS

O f all the new characters introduced in season four, Jason Carver (Mason Dye) has one of the biggest journeys. While nowhere near as villainous as Vecna or Dr Brenner, the good-looking but self-righteous jock does little to be proud of riling when up the good people of Hawkins.

Captain of the Hawkins High School basketball team and boyfriend of popular cheerleader Chrissy Cunningham, he seems to have it all. An accomplished athlete and public speaker, we first see him give a rallying speech to his team. But he has another side; he's a bully, never slow to turn on anyone he considers 'uncool' – step forward members of the Hellfire Club who he believes are 'freaks'.

So when Chrissy is murdered, by Vecna as it turns out, and Jason sees his 'perfect world' come tumbling down his nasty side comes to the fore. He already hates Eddie so accuses him of killing Chrissy, spreading a false story that the Hellfire club is a front for a satanic cult and that her death was sacrificial.

As the season goes on Jason loses all reason, refusing to believe anything other than his own invented narrative. He won't listen when Lucas tries to put him straight and, even after seeing his friend Patrick being killed by Vecna, still puts it down to Eddie – claiming that he was somehow channelling satanic power. Even though he loses Chrissy and Patrick, and comes to a gruesome end himself, it's hard to find much sympathy for Jason who represents all that was so wrong about the real 1980s 'satanic panic'.

CREATURES OF THE UPSIDE DOWN

THIS WORLD IS HOME TO SOME DANGEROUS RESIDENTS. YOU BETTER HOPE YOU DON'T MEET THESE CREEPY CREATURES ON A DARK NIGHT

Existing parallel to our world, the Upside Down is a dimension that defines danger. As you take uneasy steps across its stagnant environment, you might find friendly locales like Castle Byers or the library. Don't let that familiarity fool you, however. The Upside Down is uncanny, unpleasant and unwelcoming, and you'd do well to stay far, far away.

This alien landscape is home to grotesque abominations that consider humans their prey. These creatures only exist to kill and dominate – there is no reasoning with them, no bargaining; all you can do is run, fight back, or perish.

Our world became entangled with the Upside Down in 1983 when the scientists at Hawkins National Laboratory created a gateway between the two worlds. The scientists discovered that one of their test subjects – Eleven – had encountered an otherworldly creature in an experiment. In forcing the girl to make contact with this being, a rift was created, and the entity called a Demogorgon stumbled through.

This was the first known incursion of a creature from the Upside Down entering our world, and it would not be the last. We later learn that there is an intelligent and malevolent force pulling the strings. One which has designs on our world and will stop at nothing to dominate the human race. The creatures of the Upside Down are still enshrouded in mystery. However, here are the entities we know and what they're capable of...

Above: The Demogorgon unfurls its flower-like maw to reveal row upon row of terrifying teeth.

"As vicious as they are, the Demogorgons are far from the most menacing lifeform of the Upside Down"

THE DEMOGORGON

The first creature of the Upside Down we encounter in the *Stranger Things* canon is the Demogorgon. It's also the species of monster we know the most about, having explored its entire life cycle across three seasons. It's a tall, grey, thin humanoid figure with super-strong elongated limbs and a featureless face. The stuff of nightmares, basically. And that featureless head? It unfurls like a flower, revealing rows of sharp teeth and a gaping maw. The Demogorgon is named after a Dungeons & Dragons monster. In the tabletop game, it's a powerful fiend that defeats Will Byers' in-game character, foreshadowing his abduction in the real world.

This creature is truly not of this world, uncanny, uncaring and nigh-on unstoppable. That escaped Demogorgon from Hawkins Lab we mentioned earlier gets beaten, shot and set on fire, yet it still manages to draw breath until Eleven obliterates it with her psychic powers.

It acts as an instinctive predator, killing what it deems to be prey, yet it appears to have desires beyond this. Instead of killing him, it abducts Will Byers and cocoons him in the Upside Down, perhaps to use him to create another Demogorgon in a Xenomorph-style reproductive ritual.

Sticking with the Xenomorph comparison, much like the star from the *Alien* films, the Demogorgon goes through different forms throughout its life. We have Dustin Henderson to thank for this information, as he attempts to keep one of these otherworldly horrors as a pet, and we get to watch it grow.

The first stage looks like a chunky slug and potentially requires a host to grow. After his ordeal in the Upside Down, Will coughs one of these up into his bathroom sink.

Stage two, or the 'Pollywog', looks similar to a newt... or, you know, a pollywog. Here, we can see an instinct to feed kick in. Dustin's creature, Dart, steals candy and rummages around trash cans, for example. A fear of fire also surfaces at this point.

The third stage clearly resembles a frog. The monster's skin turns a bottle-green, it grows rapidly and fully walks on its four legs. You'll start to see tiny rows of pointed teeth at this stage, too. Perhaps this cute thing is not that friendly, after all?

Stages four and five are fairly similar to each other. Here, the Demogorgon resembles a slimy alien cat or dog... only instead of a cute furry face, it has that god-awful mouth flower. After the fifth stage of growth is complete, the Demogorgon becomes bigger, bipedal and fully develops into that gross beastie we know and love. Gorgeous.

THE MIND FLAYER

As vicious as they are, the Demogorgons are far from the most menacing lifeform of the Upside Down. That honour belongs to the Mind Flayer, a Lovecraftian aberration of gigantic proportions. Even its name elicits a feeling of existential dread: this creature will peel away everything about you until there is nothing left. Again, this creature is named after a similarly grotesque D&D creature, one that takes great pride in devouring the brains of other humanoid creatures.

Unlike the Demogorgons that appear to operate purely on instinct, the Mind Flayer is intelligent. It schemes, manipulates and is highly hostile to the human race. We

Left: A gateway to the Upside Down – an unpleasant and unwelcoming parallel world.

only ever see the creature in the Upside Down, from the perspective of Will Byers, who shares a connection with the entity. It is massive; hundreds of feet tall, and its body comprises an ethereal, smoke-like substance. It stands astride multiple tendrils that split off into countless 'legs', resembling the roots and webbing that coat the entirety of its homeworld. At the centre of its tangle is a long, featureless head.

While its form is imposing, the Mind Flayer does not demonstrate any obvious physical threat like its Demogorgon sibling. Rather, this creature's weapon of choice is its psychic powers. It can dominate the minds of humans, twisting them and turning them into 'the Flayed'. We see the Mind Flayer attempt this with Will Byers, as it influences his mind making the sweet boy hostile to his friends and family. We also see it hold full control over the Demogorgons, ordering them to enact its will.

This mastermind's true motivations are unknown. Through his possession, Will offers a glimpse of the creature's plans. Speaking through Will, it tells us that it wishes to merge the Upside Down and our world together, granting it a larger dominion for it to rule over. Viewing itself as an apex predator, it will likely not stop until it dominates every living creature it can.

The Mind Flayer can also alter organic material and create proxies to do its bidding in our world. After the gate between worlds is reopened by Russian agents operating

Left: Billy finds himself possessed by the Mind Flayer.

Right: Hopper explores the underground tunnels of the Upside Down.

in Hawkins, the Mind Flayer dominates a group of rats and humans, morphing their matter into a real-world avatar. We see an even lesser, 'fleshy' version of the creature appear in Hawkins Hospital, created from a pair of Flayed humans with the objective of killing Nancy Wheeler and Jonathan Byers. This iteration of the Mind Flayer is crab-like, rabid and susceptible to the remarkable superhuman powers of Eleven.

While the Mind Flayer is supremely powerful, it's not unstoppable. As with other creatures of the Upside Down, it holds an impulsive fear of fire and extends this phobia to its Flayed hosts. By placing a Flayed Will in a heated environment – surrounded by heaters and blankets – the Mind Flayer squirms in pain and discomfort, and ultimately tears itself from Will's body.

The victories against the Mind Flayer have been small and probably insignificant in the grand scheme of things. It still has plans for our world, and will likely regroup and return, perhaps more powerful than before.

THE SPIDER MONSTER

The Mind Flayer casts a long shadow over Hawkins, but its true form only operates from its home realm, the Upside Down. Instead of entering our world, it chooses to operate through proxies. The 'Spider Monster' residing in the derelict steel works building is one of the Mind Flayer's avatars, and it is one heck of a grotesque monster.

Constructed from the flesh of Flayed rats and humans, the Mind Flayer twists organic matter from the creatures it dominates into its own image: an arachnid-like being with sinewy appendages. It has one objective: kill Eleven, the one person standing between the Mind Flayer and Hawkins.

It's not as imposing as its 'parent'. The Spider Monster stands at around 30 feet tall, with bones and teeth sticking out of its gross form. While the Mind Flayer is a creature evolved to fight mental battles, the Spider Monster is a physical powerhouse. Strong, vile and dangerous, it's a huge threat to the heroes of Hawkins.

Threatening as it might be, this is still a creature that requires an open connection to the Upside Down – and so the Mind Flayer – to survive. Once Jim Hopper destroyed the Russian-built gateway to the otherworldly dimension, the Mind Flayer's influence was severed, and so the Spider Monster melted away.

Right: Eleven defeated a Demogorgon in *Stranger Things'* first season.

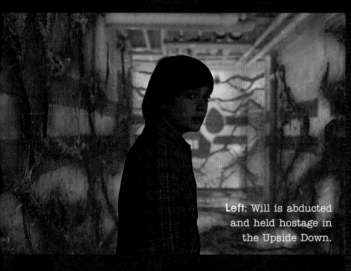

Left: Will is abducted and held hostage in the Upside Down.

Left: Steve battles the Demogorgon with his spiked bat.

THE FLAYED

Though they're 'technically' still human, the thralls of the Mind Flayer are so far removed from the people they once were it's difficult to see them as anything but monsters. The Flayed are stripped of all their worldly wants and desires, and only exist to serve the hive mind.

The Mind Flayer's influence twists its hosts' insides, and Flayed creatures no longer eat food. Instead, the Mind Flayer prefers that they consume poisonous chemicals like fertiliser and washing powder. A Flayed's blood turns a dark, tar-like colour too, which can be seen from their gross varicose veins.

A Flayed is nothing but a tool to the Mind Flayer; a being to be contorted to its master's ends. As such, the mastermind of the Upside Down can break down a Flayed into a fleshy sludge, morphing its thralls together into something much more insidious. We see this with the 'Spider Monster', being formed under the Hawkins steelworks, constructed from the flesh of hundreds of Flayed humans and rats.

As hopeless as it might seem, a Flayed can regain its humanity. Will Byers is fully rescued from the Mind Flayer's grasp, and while potentially too far gone to be fully saved, a Flayed Billy Hargrove regains his faculties just in time to save his sister and her friends.

VECNA

Horrendous new Upside Down monster Vecna (Jamie Campbell Bower) was introduced as the main antagonist of season four. The humanoid chap is eventually, revealed to be Henry Creel, an escapee from Dr Brenner's Hawkins' Lab and the real perpetrator of the murders of all the test subjects previously blamed on Eleven, plus every other disaster since the start. He became a monster after a showdown with Eleven during which she sent him through a gate to the Upside Down where the harsh conditions there gradually transformed him into Vecna, creator of the Mind Flayer. Turns out he'd been acting through his Mind Flayer creation in the previous seasons. Now taking a more direct approach, Vecna is a formidable foe, responsible for a new series of murders in Hawkins, using those deaths to open new gates. The group's efforts to defeat him, both physically and psychically, form the major story arc of the season.

SEASON ONE

MEET THE CAST – AND CREATURE! – THAT STARTED IT ALL. DO YOU DARE ENTER THE UPSIDE DOWN?

Welcome to the dark but wonderful universe of season one of *Stranger Things*, the eight classic episodes from 2016 that set up the show's six-year run to date. From the moment that we find ourselves transported to the picture-postcard town of Hawkins, Indiana, in late 1983, we're placed directly into the centre of a web of characters, all leading very different lives, but all about to be drawn into a terrifying drama that is unlike any we've witnessed before.

Created by Ross and Matt Duffer, who learned their craft from *The Sixth Sense* director M. Night Shyamalan, *Stranger Things* was utterly convincing for viewers of any age. Older fans who remembered the Eighties responded to the Duffer brothers' warm portrayal of pre-internet, pre-cellphone life in the suburbs, but you don't need to be aged over 40 to enjoy the vibes from that simpler age. Besides, who doesn't empathise with the gang of misfit kids at the heart of the *Stranger Things* universe? After all, we *were* those kids.

No wonder this amazing new show became a must-watch that year, competing with Netflix's established programming and scooping a ton of positive reviews from the critics. Suddenly, everyone wanted in on the *Stranger Things* phenomenon. Let's look back and remind ourselves how it unfolded...

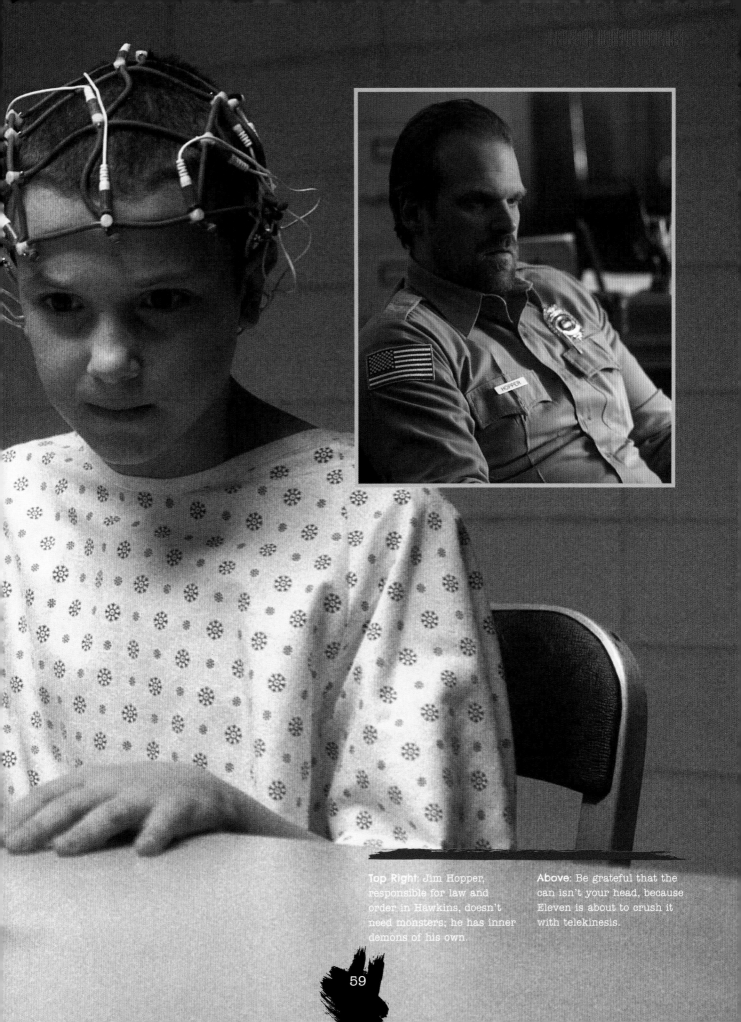

Top Right: Jim Hopper, responsible for law and order in Hawkins, doesn't need monsters; he has inner demons of his own.

Above: Be grateful that the can isn't your head, because Eleven is about to crush it with telekinesis.

CHAPTER ONE:
THE VANISHING OF WILL BYERS

Don't all epic TV shows start with an unforgettable opening scene? In the case of *Stranger Things*' first episode, you'll never forget the moment that we enter a government-owned science facility in the – sadly fictional – town of Hawkins, Indiana. This being November 1983, when digital watches were pretty much the most advanced technology around, you won't see any recognisably modern gadgetry. As we look around the spooky facility, we know from the first few seconds that we really shouldn't be in here. This certainty deepens when a scientist is attacked by some horrendous-sounding monster: we say horrendous-'sounding', because in true sci-fi-horror style, we don't get to see the nasty thing yet.

We then meet Will Byers (Noah Schnapp), a local 12-year-old who is about to leave the weekly Dungeons

& Dragons session that he plays with his friends Mike Wheeler (Finn Wolfhard), Dustin Henderson (Gaten Matarazzo) and Lucas Sinclair (Caleb McLaughlin). As he cycles home, he meets the mysterious creature, which has escaped the lab and is on the hunt for prey.

Cut to *Stranger Things*' most sympathetic adults, Will's mother Joyce (Winona Ryder) and police chief Jim Hopper (David Harbour). As Joyce begs Jim to search for her missing son, we begin to learn more about the characters' circumstances: both have suffered serious trauma in their pasts, snippets of which are hinted at in this opening episode.

Back in the forbidding government lab, its intimidating director Dr Martin Brenner (Matthew Modine) has discovered some strange-looking goop oozing out of the basement, and as we know from all classic Eighties horror, it's never a good idea to go down to the basement. Still, he has other things on his mind, not least the fact that a girl – as yet unidentified – has managed to escape the lab. Grimly, he orders her pursuit.

The runaway kid herself, wearing a hospital gown and a

Left: Before the beast came: Will Byers goes about his day, unaware of the events that are about to overtake him.

Above: The gang face their deepest fears in night-time Hawkins, Indiana: (from left) Lucas, Mike, Eleven and Dustin.

terrified expression, enters a diner, where the owner Benny finds a tattoo on her arm that reads '011'. Eleven, played by Millie Bobby Brown, is all set to be rescued by social services and head off to a happy life when agents sent by Dr Brenner – who has tapped the local phone lines – burst in and kill poor Benny. Using telekinesis, Eleven evades their clutches and escapes into the woods, where she is discovered by Mike, Dustin and Lucas.

Meanwhile, Joyce's landline rings. She picks up, only to hear garbled noises that she thinks might be coming from her missing son. Is it really Will, and if so, where the heck is he calling from?

CHAPTER TWO:
THE WEIRDO ON MAPLE STREET

What happens when you come across a homeless waif in the woods? If you're kind-hearted souls like Mike, Dustin and Lucas, you bring her home, sneak her into your room and set her up with a comfy den to sleep in while you debate what on earth to do with her. Mike suggests that they confide in his mum, but Eleven is vehemently against this, warning that 'bad men' are trying to find her – as indeed they are. We don't want that to happen, spooked as we are by what happened to Benny and unnerved by the evil Dr Brenner.

It's time to meet some new characters, the first of which is Will's brother Jonathan (Charlie Heaton), an intense but sweet-natured kid who refuses to give up on his missing sibling. He asks his dad Lonnie (Ross Partridge) for help, but – classic absent father that he is – Lonnie is no use. We're also introduced to Mike's sister Nancy (Natalia Dyer) and her friend Barbara 'Barb' Holland (Shannon Purser), the first of which is accompanied by a jock boyfriend, Steve Harrington (Joe Keery).

Meanwhile, the search for Eleven intensifies, with Hopper's search party finding a bit of her hospital gown near

Right: When a kid loses his BMX, you know bad things are happening, even if you're Hopper's less-than-professional search team.

the lab she escaped from, raising Hopper's suspicions. Eleven herself helps the boys out with their search for Will, blowing their minds with a demonstration of her telekinetic powers: a key moment in this episode comes when she uses their Dungeons & Dragons board to tell them that Will is on the 'Upside Down' side of the board. Worse, she tells them that he is in danger thanks to the terrible Demogorgon, a Dungeons & Dragons character whose name they apply to the monster that abducted him.

Just to creep us out even more, when Nancy, Steve and Barb go to a party and Jonathan photographs them in secret, he witnesses Barb sitting by the pool – before she suddenly vanishes, having been attacked by the Demogorgon. Back at Joyce's house, the phone rings, music starts to play on Will's stereo, and the creature itself begins to emerge through the wall. Help!

CHAPTER THREE:
HOLLY, JOLLY

If you thought all that was scary, *Stranger Things* is just getting started. First of all, poor old Barb wakes up, having lost consciousness while being kidnapped by the pool – and who can blame her? Unfortunately, much as we're rooting for her to wake up in her own bed, there's no such luck for Barb – because she's in the Upside Down.

It's hard to explain what the Upside Down is, except to say that it's some sort of parallel dimension that you never, ever want to visit. A cross between the xenomorphs' terrifying hive in *Aliens* and the lonely, windswept heath

in *Macbeth* where those horrible witches hang out, the Upside Down is less of a destination and more of a hallucination. Sadly, there's no escape for Barb, who is stalked by the Upside Down's resident monster, the Demogorgon.

Left: Get on your bikes and ride: in hot pursuit of the gang's missing friend, Will Byers.

Above: You wouldn't like her when she's angry: Eleven focuses her mental powers with destruction in mind.

"It's hard to explain what the Upside Down is, except to say that it's some sort of parallel dimension that you never, ever want to visit"

Meanwhile, back in the real world, Joyce is out of her mind – or is she? – with grief for her missing son Will, having started to believe that he's communicating with her via lightbulb fluctuations in her home. Meanwhile, Hopper has scheduled a meeting with the wholly untrustworthy Dr Brenner, who shows him fake security footage from the time when Will vanished.

Diligent police officer that he is, Hopper isn't buying any of this, and does a bit of investigation. He unearths Brenner's connection to a previous CIA experiment called Project

MKUltra that involved brainwashing subjects with drugs, and also an accusation that Brenner had kidnapped a young girl. In a related scene, Eleven reveals that Brenner was indeed her jailer, and that he once punished her when she declined to use her powers to harm a cat.

Elsewhere, Nancy narrowly escapes from an encounter with the Demogorgon, and Joyce receives a message from Will via an alphabetic board on her wall that says 'Run!' Just as we relax, safe in the knowledge that Will is alive, his body is pulled from a lake in a quarry.

CHAPTER FOUR:
THE BODY

Believe us, you want a mum as cool as Joyce, who refuses to believe that the body found in the lake is actually that of her son Will, despite all evidence being to the contrary. No one else believes her stories of Will communicating with her through lightbulbs, but does that stop her? Heck no.

The plot thickens when Eleven convinces Mike that Will's voice can be heard through his toy walkie-talkie, leading the gang to speculate that they can connect to Will more reliably if they use the amateur radio at their school to talk to him. But how will they make this happen? Never underestimate the power of teenage ingenuity.

Not everyone is having as good a time as they are. Finding a photo of Barb that Jonathan took at the party where she disappeared, Nancy notices a rather

Above: Who needs school when there's a supernatural monster to track down? Mike and Lucas crack the books.

Right: Joyce Byers is the mum everybody wants to have their back: she'll stop at nothing to protect her boys.

unpleasant figure approaching her late friend in the picture. Yes, it's the Demogorgon, which Jonathan has heard about from Joyce – herself informed of the evil beastie's existence through Will's communications – leading him to realise that his mum has been right all along. Nancy's boyfriend Steve fails to grasp the importance of all of this, of course, and they fall out.

Our man Hopper, who deserves a medal by this point, is starting to get suspicious about more or less everything that is going on – to the extent that he applies a severe beating to the state trooper who found Will in the lake. This approach is crude but effective, leading the trooper to admit that he's been ordered to lie about the discovery of the boy's body. Hopper then sneaks into the morgue where Will is lying in state, and who would have thought it, the body turns out to be a fake. Now we're all hopeful that Will is alive again.

But where is he? Fortunately, Eleven and the boys sneak into their school, fire up the ham radio and tune into Will sending messages to Joyce. At her house, Joyce tears away the wallpaper – and sees Will caught in the eerie netherworld behind it.

CHAPTER FIVE:
THE FLEA AND THE ACROBAT

Hopper is still snooping around the lab in the wake of his discovery, and finds the same mysterious goo that was concerning Dr Brenner a while back. Unfortunately he is discovered by the lab guards, who knock him out – proving beyond reasonable doubt that something highly dodgy is going on.

This being the early Eighties, popular science was something that obsessed all right-thinking teenagers. While racking their brains about the possibility of Will communicating with Joyce from an alternate dimension, the boys quiz their friendly science teacher Mr Clarke

Left: One by one, many of Hawkins' citizens face the terror of the Upside Down.

69

about the idea of crossing from one dimension to another. He raises the idea that a gate between these different universes might well exist, with the kids realising that such a gate might well mess with the electromagnetic field of Earth. In that case, what better tool than a magnetic compass, every boy scout's favourite accessory?

Meanwhile, Hopper suddenly wakes up, back at his house. He experiences a Eureka moment when he comes across a hidden microphone and realises that pretty much everything he thought was right was wrong. He's now fully on board with Joyce and her insistence that Will is still around somewhere, even if that somewhere isn't in our dimension.

Talking of which, the gang have been following their compasses around the local countryside in an attempt to locate the gate that will allow them to rescue Will. There's a problem with this plan, though, because Eleven fears that the success of their search will mean she has to encounter the Demogorgon. We learn more about this awful creature in a flashback, when Eleven's memories reveal that she went toe-to-toe with the horrid thing while undergoing one of Brenner's misguided experiments. Trying to avoid this, she messes telekinetically with the boys' compasses. This annoys Lucas, who fights Mike, although Eleven uses mind control to pull them apart, and runs off.

Nancy and Jonathan are also trying to track down the Demogorgon, with rather more success. While searching in the forest, they come across a deer, which they follow through a gate that leads – you guessed it – to the Upside Down. Uh-oh.

CHAPTER SIX:
THE MONSTER

It's time to discover the link between Eleven and the deadly Demogorgon, and in this episode, that finally happens.

Fortunately for Nancy, she doesn't end up as the Demogorgon's dinner, being pulled out of the Upside Down by Jonathan before the creature can grab her. Thoroughly spooked by the experience, she doesn't want

to sleep alone that night, and asks Jonathan if he'll stay in her room overnight. You can't exactly blame her: if you or I had been through this experience, we'd be on the next flight out of Indiana.

Unfortunately, Steve the idiot boyfriend – who is keen to make up with her after their row a while back – sees her and Jonathan through her bedroom window and totally misinterprets the situation, with the two teenage boys ending up having a good old-fashioned fist-fight. Afterwards, Nancy and Jonathan gather weapons with which to combat the Demogorgon, speculating that the beast is attracted by blood.

Remember when the spooky Dr Brenner was accused of kidnapping someone's daughter? That someone turns out to be a woman called Terry Ives, who is comatose and being looked after by her sister Becky. Joyce and Hopper visit Terry, and Becky explains that her sister had been a participant in Project MKUltra, not knowing that she was pregnant at the time. Becky believes that Terry's baby, a girl named Jane, was kidnapped by Brenner at birth, the evil doctor planning to exploit Jane's remarkable mental powers.

We switch to Eleven, who confirms Becky's story – and her own true identity as Jane Ives – after stealing a ton of snacks from a grocery store. Hey, even masters of telekinesis have to eat. While trying to find her, Mike and Dustin are faced with a gang of bullies who are keen to gain revenge after a previous humiliation at Eleven's hands. Eleven rescues them, breaking one thug's arm with a satisfying crunch in doing so.

It's time for a full confession, and back at Mike's house, Eleven finally explains to the boys that she has some serious history with the Demogorgon. While trapped by Brenner at the lab, she was obliged to make contact with the monster for reasons best known to the good doctor: in doing so, she accidentally opened the gate to the Upside Down, allowing the Demogorgon to enter our dimension and start killing people. What's saddest about this is that Eleven, or rather Jane, feels that it's all her fault.

As she talks, Brenner's agents surround Mike's house...

Above: Eleven's arrival in the lives of the gang has an impact on each of the members.

Above: Eleven discovers her love of Eggos

CHAPTER SEVEN:
THE BATHTUB

In a tight spot, Mike, Dustin and Eleven run away from the house. The agents pursue them, but Eleven takes care of this by flipping one of their vehicles over. This blocks the pursuers' path, and the kids are safe. For now.

By now, the truth of the whole supernatural situation has become apparent to everybody. Nancy and Jonathan explain that they know about the Demogorgon to Joyce and Hopper, and in a meeting of everyone that we now know and love, they gather to discuss plans. Realising at last that Eleven is actually Jane Ives, the gang asks her to use her telepathy to search for Will and Barb, both of who they hope to be alive in the Upside Down.

But it's not quite as simple as that, unfortunately. Eleven

"Hearts broke across the viewing audience when it was revealed that Barb had died, but this was a necessary plot development"

doesn't have infinite sources of energy, and is severely weakened by her defence of the group against the agents. The boys agree that to boost her powers, they will need to find a solution. Science comes to their rescue once again as they break into school and assemble a structure similar to a sensory-deprivation tank, in which Eleven can recuperate, ready to focus her powers once more on finding their lost friends.

Once her energy is restored, Eleven locates Barb in the Upside Down. Hearts broke across a viewing audience of millions when it was revealed that Barb has died, but this was a necessary plot development: how else would we feel that the Demogorgon is really dangerous, and that it must be defeated at all costs?

Eleven also finds Will, who – to our relief – is alive, although he's clinging on for dear life, hiding in the Upside Down equivalent of the fort that he built in their back yard. The question now is how to rescue him. Fortunately, the gang quickly deduces that the gate which gives access to that dimension must be in the basement of Dr Brenner's lab. Hopper and Joyce duly break into the facility, but are arrested by security guards.

Is it game over? Not yet, as Nancy and Jonathan have a cunning plan. They'd better execute it quickly though, because in the Upside Down, the Demogorgon has located Will's fort and is starting to break in.

CHAPTER EIGHT:
THE UPSIDE DOWN

Our terrifying tale draws to a close – for now – but perhaps not in the way we expect. Our hero Hopper, conflicted and haunted by the death of his daughter many years before, has always been a complex character, and he demonstrates this by revealing Eleven's location to Dr Brenner. In return, Brenner allows him and Joyce to enter the Upside Down to attempt to rescue Will.

In a parallel scene, Nancy and Jonathan are planning to attract the monster themselves by cutting their hands, as it loves the scent of blood. The monster appears as soon as the claret starts to flow, as does Nancy's former beau Steve, who intends to apologise for fighting Jonathan. There's no time for apologies, though, as the three youths launch into combat against the dreaded Demogorgon, managing to set the monster on fire.

Brenner and his goons burst into the school where Eleven and the boys are hiding, but his plans are somewhat thwarted when she uses her powers to wipe out most of his agents – clearly the sensory-deprivation tank was a splendid idea. Brenner's day is spoiled even more when the Demogorgon suddenly appears and kills him. With one last blast of telekinetic energy, Eleven blows the creature to smithereens, but apparently at the cost of her own life, as she disappears with it.

In the Upside Down, Hopper and Joyce find Will: he may have avoided the Demogorgon, but he's been left with a strange tentacle down his throat. They revive him and bring him back to the real world, where he recovers in hospital.

So everything is fine in the end, it seems. A month later, Will vomits up a repulsive slug-like organism, but that can't be significant… can it?

Right: Dr Brenner presents a civilised front, but in reality he is the cause of the majority of Eleven's problems.

SEASON TWO

THE PLOT THICKENS AS WE HEAD INTO SEASON 2 OF STRANGER THINGS. WILL WE SURVIVE THE UPSIDE DOWN A SECOND TIME?

After a debut season as successful as that of *Stranger Things*, the show was poised to take the world by storm in 2017 – and so it did, breaking records and becoming the most popular streamed original programme on the planet. Audiences and critics alike lined up to heap praise on the development of the story, which amped up the fear of the original run and expanded its universe with cool new characters.

What was most noticeable about season two was its ambition: having set the scene so successfully, the Duffer brothers could have rested on their laurels and essentially repeated themselves, had they so chosen. Not a bit of it: they considered how the *Stranger Things* world could grow, planned trajectories for the characters and made them interact in ways that we hadn't considered.

We get to learn a lot more about a particular central character who we thought was no longer with us (any guesses?) and of course, we're forced to deal with a terrific new monster – although 'terrifying' might be a more appropriate adjective, now we come to think of it.

CHAPTER ONE:
MADMAX

Given the nightmarish nature of the terrifying events of the previous year, by the fall of 1984 the residents of Hawkins, Indiana, are still struggling to come to terms with their encounter with the Demogorgon. In particular, Mike Wheeler and his sister Nancy are grieving for the tragic losses of Eleven and Barb. Still, life can and must go on, with the old gang – Mike, his returned brother Will, Dustin and Lucas – returning to school and being captivated by a new arrival, Maxine 'Max' Mayfield (Sadie Sink).

It's Halloween, and while the town prepares for the coolest night of the year, there's less comfortable stuff going on in Pittsburgh, Pennsylvania. A bank robbery is underway, led by a girl with interesting psychic powers – and a tattoo on her arm that reads 008. Does anything sound familiar about this?

Meanwhile, Joyce Byers is in a new relationship with her old school chum, Bob Newby (Sean Astin), and Hopper is still investigating odd occurrences around the town, namely a field of rotting pumpkins. A new character called Murray Bauman (Brett Gelman), a conspiracy theorist, has heard rumours about what happened in Hawkins the previous year, and is hunting for evidence that might back up his classic Eighties-era theory – that Eleven was a spy sent by the Russians to undermine life in good ol' America.

When season one ended, Will Byers coughed up a repulsive slug of some sort, implying that his travails aren't quite over yet, and indeed he starts our new season hallucinating about a massive monster with tentacles – like the Demogorgon, but even worse, if you can imagine it. Joyce and Hopper speculate that Will is experiencing post-traumatic stress disorder, and take him – guess where? – back to the government lab where it all started.

Yes, this sounds illogical, not to say suicidal, especially as we learn that the gate to the Upside Down in the basement is not only still there, it's expanding, much to the concern of the lab's new boss, Dr Sam Owens. Sci-fi

Top: Back in action after we all thought she was Demogorgon fodder, Eleven is tougher than ever in season two.

Right: Hopper is back to being a hero – although this time he is the one who ends up needing rescuing.

fans will be unnerved to see that Owens is played by Paul Reiser, who was also the villainous Carter Burke in *Aliens*, but the good doctor appears to be a decent chap, so we can relax.

Nancy and her returned boyfriend Steve go and have dinner with Barb's parents, who are convinced that their daughter is alive. So sure are they that they've hired the aforementioned conspiracy nut Murray to search for her.

So all is far from tranquil in Hawkins, Indiana, it seems – but a bigger shock awaits us. Returning to the cabin in the woods where he now lives, Hopper reveals that he has a new housemate: a teenage girl whose hair has now grown out a little and whose name is Eleven. Yes, we punched the air when we saw her – and you did too.

CHAPTER TWO:
TRICK OR TREAT, FREAK

Fortunately, we're given some explanation for Eleven's reappearance: flashbacks show us that she survived the death of the Demogorgon, escaping from the Upside Down and then being pursued by a gang of agents. Hopper provided her with sanctuary, but she's not quite ready to go 'full recluse' just yet, and wants to go trick or treating with her buddies. Sensibly, Hopper refuses, as he's brokering a deal with Dr Owens that will allow her to return to society. In any case, he has other things to worry about, such as a whole town full of rotten pumpkins – caused, he discovers, by the same sticky goo that he once found at the lab.

Elsewhere, Nancy and Steve are arguing again. She wants to 'fess up to Barb's parents about what really happened to their daughter, but Steve – reasonably enough – feels that this would be a bad idea. At a Halloween party, she has one too many cocktails and yells at him for being unsympathetic. Those two, eh?

Right: Kids today, eh? You don't know if they're cleaning up the streets or chasing down a monster from another world.

Above: Lucas Sinclair and the girl that the whole school is talking about, Max Mayfield: crazy older brother not pictured.

Right: Nancy and Jonathan are grabbed by Dr Owens and his goons as they try to reach out to Barb's mother.

CHAPTER THREE:
THE POLLYWOG

Joyce's boyfriend Bob is a nice guy, and wants Will to get better, so he urges the lad to face up to his fears – although we can safely assume that Bob doesn't know that Will isn't just scared of the dark, he's actually in mortal terror of a giant slavering demon.

More bad advice in this episode comes from Nancy, who persuades Jonathan that it would be an outstanding idea if they told Barb's parents the truth about what happened to their daughter: they arrange to meet them the following day, worrying that Owens might be tapping the phones, as his late predecessor Brenner did. Owens himself is in trouble with Hopper, who thinks that the lab is responsible for the sludge that is destroying the local pumpkins.

Dustin's little buddy from the trashcan resembles a slug of some kind: apparently not spooked by the arrival of yet another creepy organism, he nicknames it D'Artagnan ('Dart') and takes it to meet his buddies. They conclude that it's from the Upside Down, as Will recognises the noise it makes from his ongoing hallucinations. Why they don't stamp on it immediately is not made clear.

Bored of being stuck in Hopper's cabin in the woods, Eleven sneaks out and goes to see Mike. Seeing him chatting with new girl Max at the school, she assumes the two are flirting and leaves, saddened by what she has witnessed. The love-story subplot and the horror plotline are weaving neatly in and out of each other at this point: nice writing, Duffer brothers.

"Seeing Mike chatting with new girl Max at school, Eleven assumes the two are flirting and leaves, saddened by what she has witnessed"

Meanwhile, Will's hallucinations are getting worse, and he confides in Mike. The two discuss the situation, and Mike reveals that he's been trying to contact Eleven. At the same time, Eleven is trying to establish communications with Mike, with no luck.

We end the episode with an unpleasant surprise for Dustin, who returns home from trick-or-treating to find a strange-looking creature in his dustbin. This can't bode well.

During another terrifying hallucination about the tentacled monster, Will heeds Bob's friendly if ill-advised tips and goes toe-to-toe with the beast. This doesn't work out in his favour, as it grabs him and jams one of its tendrils down his throat. You'd think the poor kid would have suffered enough by now…

CHAPTER FOUR:
WILL THE WISE

Fortunately, Will is revived by Joyce and his buddies, and is apparently well enough to go home – although when he gets there, he starts exhibiting some bizarre behaviour, drawing weird designs on paper and asking that the house be kept at an ice-cold temperature. Hopper comes over to investigate, and together they figure out that his drawings line up to represent vine-like plants.

We're given much more of an insight into the character of Dr Owens in this episode. His goons grab Nancy and Jonathan when they try to connect with Barb's mother, and take them to the government lab. Here, Owens comes clean about the gate to the Upside Down, which now looks even less welcoming than it did before, and admits that Barb died in there. However, he wants to keep foreign governments from finding out about it – probably wisely, given the circumstances. Once Nancy and Jonathan are

allowed to leave, the former reveals that she caught all of Owens' confession on tape – a resourceful move.

It all goes badly pear-shaped at this point, with Lucas trying to get friendly with Max, only to be prevented from doing so by her psychopathic big brother, Billy Hargrove (Dacre Montgomery). Eleven and Hopper have a massive row about her leaving his cabin, which ends when she blows out the windows in telekinetic anger. Cleaning up the broken glass the next day, she discovers evidence that Terry Ives is her biological mother, and attempts to contact her using her mind powers.

The bad news we were all expecting comes when Dustin discovers that his pet slug Dart has escaped its cage, breakfasted on the family cat and evolved into a baby Demogorgon. He can't say he wasn't warned, can he? It all gets even worse when Hopper, digging up some decaying pumpkins, discovers a tunnel that leads directly to the Upside Down.

CHAPTER FIVE:
DIG DUG

"Wait! Don't go down there!" we all shout at the screen as Hopper enters the dread tunnel to the Upside Down, and we're absolutely right to do so, because he soon gets stuck and faints. Fortunately for him, Will experiences a vision that reveals Hopper's whereabouts, assisted by Joyce's boyfriend Bob, who interprets Will's hallucination and identifies the pumpkin field where the over-enthusiastic police officer was last seen.

We now get to spend some time with the keen conspiracy theorist Murray, who listens to the tape of Owens' confessions made by Nancy. He correctly thinks that no one will believe any of it, but that perhaps an edited version of events might encourage people to investigate. In fact, it's fessing-up time all round, as the lovelorn Lucas reveals all about what happened to Will to his crush, Max. Meanwhile, the gang are trying to catch Dart, trapping the newborn monster in Dustin's basement – but remember, in *Stranger Things*, things never work out well in basements.

Back to Eleven, who finds out where her mother Terry and her aunt Becky live, and heads over for a visit. Terry, still comatose, can be reached successfully via telekinesis, and she and her long-lost daughter communicate. Eleven learns that her mother tried to rescue her from the clutches of the evil Dr Brenner, but he zapped Terry with enough shock therapy to damage her brain, hence her

current state of catatonia. Terry also informs her that there was another girl at the lab who had psychic powers, too.

Finally, Hopper is pulled out from the tunnel to the Upside Down by Joyce, Bob, Will and Mike. Lab scientists then set the tunnels on fire for reasons best known to themselves – and the moment this happens, Will collapses to the ground in terrible pain.

CHAPTER SIX:
THE SPY

Will is in a bad way, with his memory gone and his body apparently being controlled by some invisible force. After

he's taken to the lab, Owens steps up to help, speculating that the tentacled monster of Will's hallucinations has spread like a virus into his brain. This will explain why the fire in the tunnels was so painful to Will.

Fortunately, more positive events are taking place elsewhere. Nancy and Jonathan enter into a romantic relationship, encouraged by Murray, who persuades them to admit their true feelings, and they send copies of the

Above: Karen Wheeler (Cara Buono), mother of Nancy and Mike, is blissfully unaware of what her kids are up to.

tape containing Owens' supernatural tale to newspapers around the United States.

Elsewhere, Lucas and Max join Dustin and Steve on a mission to catch Dart in an old junkyard. When their once-friendly, now-lethal slug buddy arrives, the gang see to their horror that it is accompanied by a load of half-grown monsters of the Upside Down persuasion – and while they may be adolescents rather than the fully adult and fully terrifying creatures we've met before, they're still scary. However, just as the pack of monsters is about to turn the gang of unfortunate teenagers into brunch, they suddenly change their minds and run away.

In the meantime, Owens has been considering a plan of action. Will mentions an area that he can't see, blocked off by the king monster that is controlling him, so Owens sends a team to search for it – not realising that this is what it wants all along. His team is duly overrun by the half-sized monsters, who then penetrate the lab and begin stalking their human adversaries.

CHAPTER SEVEN:
THE LOST SISTER

While our heroes await their fate in the lab at the hands of a cohort of monsters from the Upside Down, the action shifts to the Windy City of Chicago, where Eleven goes to track down the girl that her mother Terry had mentioned in their earlier telepathic chat. The girl (Linnea Berthelsen), who bears the '008' tattoo that we encountered back in episode one of this season, is called Kali: the two soon bond after realising that they were both experimented upon by Dr Brenner.

Right: Eleven further hones her abilities when she meets fellow lab subject Kali, aka 'Eight', in Chicago.

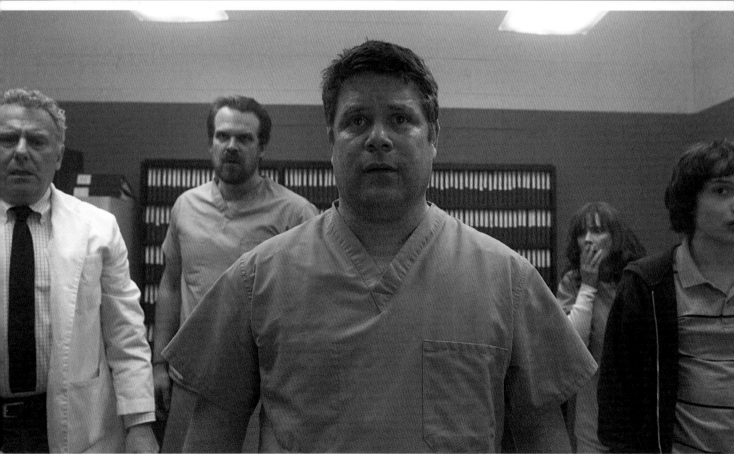

Like Eleven, Kali – or Eight, if you prefer – has led a troubled life. In Chicago, she is the leader of a street gang, and has the psychic ability to broadcast images into people's minds. She teaches Eleven that her own powers will be maximised if she learns to channel her anger. Kali's goal, to seek revenge against Brenner, is proven useless when Eleven tells her that her target is dead, so she switches her desire for revenge to Ray, the man who tortured Terry Ives.

On finding Ray at his apartment, Eleven uses her powers to choke him; as he struggles, he swears that Dr Brenner is still alive. Noticing a picture of Ray's two young daughters, she refuses to kill him, and prevents Kali from doing the same. Returning to the gang's hideout, Kali tells Eleven that she must either stay in Chicago and avenge her mother, or go back to Indiana. Eleven's decision is made for her when she suddenly experiences a vision of Mike and the Hawkins gang, trapped in Dr Owens' lab and facing down a swarm of murderous creatures.

As Kali and her gang escape from the local cops, Eleven heads for home – but will she get there in time?

CHAPTER EIGHT:
THE MIND FLAYER

All bets are off back at the lab in Hawkins. The adolescent monsters may not be as dangerous as their full-grown counterparts, but they're still plenty threatening, storming the lab and wiping out the staff. What on earth are Mike, Joyce, Hopper, Bob, Dr Owens and the unconscious Will to do?

Well, if we've learned anything from *Stranger Things*, it's that these resourceful people tend to come up with good ideas in a tight spot. While the carnage unfolds around them, they come up with the idea that Will is essentially functioning as an involuntary spy for the boss monster in the Upside Down: Mike persuades Joyce to give Will a sedative, in doing so hiding their location. Once Will is out cold, they take him to the lab's security zone to make a last stand against the invading horde.

Unfortunately, the power goes down. How will they reset

"Mike is essentially functioning as an involuntary spy for the boss monster in the Upside Down"

Left: Meet Kali and her Chicago street gang. Don't get attached, as we aren't with them for very long.

Bottom Left: We're back to the Hawkins Lab once again – although sadly, not everyone makes it out alive.

it? With a brave volunteer, in this case Bob, who sets out to reset the breakers at the power terminal. Against the odds, the resourceful fellow makes his way there and switches the power back on: this allows Mike, Joyce, Hopper and Will to escape, with Owens staying behind to guide Bob out when he gets back from his mission. Sadly for Bob, he is promptly murdered by the creatures right in front of Joyce.

The gang now reunites with Nancy, Jonathan, Steve, Dustin, Lucas and Max – in fact, more or less everybody in the series – at the Byers house, where they take a moment in order to assess the situation. Once again, Dungeons & Dragons helps to add some clarity to the proceedings, with Dustin naming the monster that controls Will the 'Mind Flayer' after a character from the game. They realise that killing it is the only option, but if they do so while it still infects Will, they'll kill him too. They manage to communicate with the comatose Will using Morse code, who instructs them to close the gate in the lab.

While they're pondering this, the Mind Flayer's creatures close in on the house: one crashes through the window, but it's dead. Who should walk in but Eleven, who has killed the rest of the monsters. Rarely has any character

CHAPTER NINE
THE GATE

With the key characters reunited, all that remains now is to kill the Mind Flayer without also killing Will, close the gate to the Upside Down, and save the entire world from being invaded by ghoulish monsters. No problem for any early Eighties pack of teenagers, you'll agree.

The plan that they cook up is as follows. First, Hopper and Eleven head to the lab to close the gate. On arrival, they meet Dr Owens, who everyone thought had died right after Bob, but got away with a few injuries. At the same time, Jonathan, Nancy and Joyce overheat Will: you'll recall that he insisted that he remain cold in the early stage of the Mind Flayer's control. Being jabbed with a red-hot poker does the trick, purging the virus from Will and leaving the rest of the gang free to kick some Flayer butt.

Next, Mike, Dustin, Lucas, Max and Steve set up a decoy movement, heading into the burned-out tunnels in an attempt to lure the pack of monsters away from the lab where Hopper and Eleven are headed. A brief distraction by Max's brother Billy, who gets into a fight with Steve, is quickly resolved, and it's game on.

Finally, Eleven and the Mind Flayer face off. It's something of a David versus Goliath situation, with the monster towering above our heroine, but she channels her anger, killing its flocks of monster soldiers and closing the gate. We breathe a sigh of relief.

Jumping forward a month, the lab has closed thanks to the newspapers who ran stories based on Nancy's tape, Barb is given a funeral, and Dr Owens fakes a birth certificate for Eleven, renaming her Jane Hopper. The kids duly attend a winter shindig at school, and it all seems pretty tranquil until we suddenly switch to the Upside Down, where the huge Mind Flayer is standing over the school, watching the kids having fun, and biding its time...

Left: Having learned about her origins, Eleven arrives back in Hawkins just in time to save the day once again.

Top: The icing on the cake of the season two finale: Eleven is allowed to attend the Snow Ball like a normal kid.

SEASON THREE

IF YOU THOUGHT THINGS IN HAWKINS WERE WEIRD BEFORE, THEY'RE ONLY JUST GETTING STARTED...

First broadcast in July 2019, the third season of *Stranger Things* had one simple mission: to extend, expand and improve upon its solid-gold first two seasons. That might sound simple to you and me, but when it comes to determining the direction of a fictional universe that has gained the love and respect of literally millions of fans worldwide, finding the right way forward is a bit like entering a gate into the Upside Down itself – fraught with missteps and easy to mess up.

Fortunately, the Duffer brothers, their cast and their crew pulled off a truly spectacular feat. Developing characters we already loved, introducing highly watchable new folks and getting them into seemingly impossible scrapes, the *Stranger Things* creative team wrote and produced arguably their most compelling season yet. Critics loved it; over 64 million households tuned into the first month of shows; and the cast became bona fide stars. However they're doing it over at *ST* HQ, they're doing it brilliantly – so let's see how it all went down!

HOPPER

CHAPTER ONE:
SUZIE, DO YOU COPY?

We open our third journey into the unsettling world of Hawkins, Indiana, with a brief flashback to June 1984, a few months before the harrowing events of season two. Who's this trying to break into the Upside Down? Why, it's a team of military scientists from the Soviet Union, America's avowed enemy at this period in history – and we have a real bad feeling about this.

Jump forward a year to the summer of 1985, and it doesn't seem that Live Aid and the release of Megadeth's debut album has left a smile on the faces of anyone in Hawkins. Instead, there's a new shopping mall called Starcourt, which is so popular that a bunch of local businesses have been forced to shut down, annoying the residents.

How is the gang doing after the last couple of years of trauma? Well, Mike and Eleven are in a relationship, although Jim Hopper – now the latter's legal dad – isn't best pleased about this. Dustin has a girlfriend, Suzie (Gabriella Pizzolo), and is using a homemade radio pylon

to communicate with her: in doing so, he picks up a garbled message in the Russian language. As for Will, he's generally troubled, fearing – accurately, as we know – that the terrible Mind Flayer is actually alive and well and about to cause problems again.

Do you remember Billy Hargrove, Max's older brother? You'll recall that in season two, he was keenly interested in hitting people. In season three, it turns out that he's also interested in hitting *on* people, namely Mike and Nancy's mother Karen. And, on the way to visit her for a "meeting of minds", he's ambushed by some form of unseen monster and dragged into a nearby mill. We already know that this is an undesirable outcome because a few minutes ago, we saw a flock of rats run into this mill and explode messily, congealing into an unsavoury lump of flesh and goo.

Top: Billy Hargrove, soon to be possessed by the Mind Flayer, makes a move on the equally enamoured Karen Wheeler.

Right: Hawkins' highly dodgy mayor, Larry Kline. Would you trust a man with that much self-assurance?

So it's business as usual in Hawkins. What are the Soviets up to? What's going to happen to Billy? And what's the significance of Starcourt Mall? All will be revealed, but it won't be pleasant.

CHAPTER TWO:
THE MALL RATS

Billy isn't having a great time in the rat-infested mill, it has to be said. The spooky, animated blob, made up of ex-rats, causes him to enter a hallucination in which he sees the Upside Down in all its horrible glory. Here, he meets his own doppelgänger and is tortured with strange visions and creepy voices. Possessed, he comes out of his trance and heads off on a mission: the unpleasant creature has convinced him to go to the swimming pool where he works as a lifeguard, kidnaps his colleague, Heather Holloway (Francesca Reale), and brings her to the mill.

Meanwhile, Nancy and Jonathan are working as interns at the local newspaper, the *Hawkins Post*. They're sent to interview an elderly local, Mrs Driscoll (Peggy Miley), who has reported that psychotic rats are eating her garden fertiliser. While they're poking around, they fail to witness a rat repeating the trick we saw at the old mill by exploding into a nasty lump of meat.

We check in briefly with the series' ongoing romantic subplot, and witness Eleven breaking up with Mike because he lied to her in order to avoid seeing her. In his defence, he did this because Hopper forced him to do so, over-worrying dad that he is. Other developments in Hawkins this week include Joyce Byers' discovery that magnetic items at home and work don't seem to be magnetic any more, a pain for any fridge-magnet collector.

We end with Dustin, Nancy's former beau Steve and a colleague called Robin Buckley (Maya 'Uma Thurman's daughter' Hawke) – who works at Starcourt Mall's ice-

Right: It's not all doom and gloom for Eleven: at heart, she's a kid like any other, who would enjoy life if the adults let her.

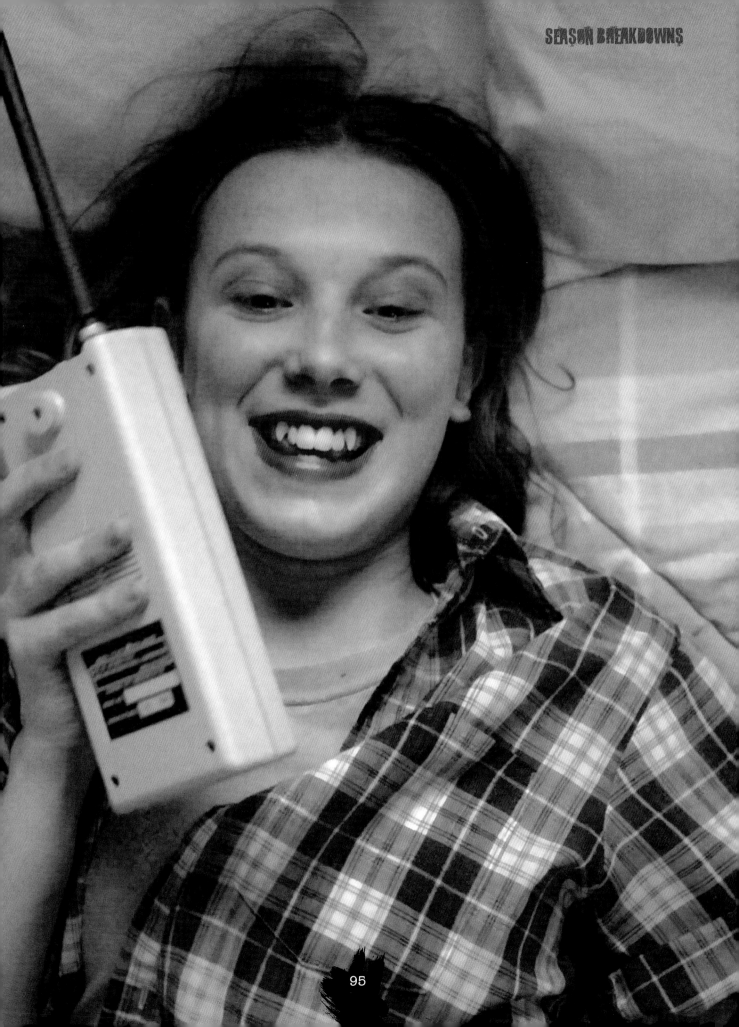

cream parlour with Steve – trying to figure out the Russian-language message that Dustin received while chatting to Suzie. Due to the Russian language not being commonly taught in Indiana high schools at this point in sociopolitical history, none of them understand it. They do figure out that it must be a code of some kind, but a code for what?

CHAPTER THREE: THE CASE OF THE MISSING LIFEGUARD

Everything escalates at an alarming pace in this episode, with plot reveals aplenty. We begin with Eleven, now boyfriend-free, who uses her telekinetic powers to see what her ex-chap Mike is up to. He isn't doing much, so she switches focus to Billy, who – as a violent sociopath possessed by the Upside Down – is a more interesting subject. His sister Max has recently discovered that he's missing, so it's a relief for her when he shows up on Eleven's mental sat-nav, but unfortunately Billy's newly acquired possession allows him to sense that Eleven is watching him. Uh-oh...

She isn't the only person finding things out in Hawkins this week. Nancy and Jonathan, the intrepid journalists,

Above: Billy finally sees the light and sacrifices himself for the greater good in the season finale.

Right: Strange things are afoot in Hawkins, Indiana, with Eleven (far right) in command of terrifying mental powers.

are now hearing multiple reports of garden fertiliser being stolen from households and rats behaving oddly. Visiting Mrs Driscoll again, they witness the senior citizen munching on some fertiliser herself, a disturbing development by anyone's standards.

The 'evil Russians' trope of so much Eighties sci-fi is now fully up and running, with Robin decoding the mysterious transmission and revealing that a shipment from the Soviet Union is about to arrive at Starcourt Mall that evening; later, she, Steve and Dustin witness a posse of gun-toting Russian military arriving with said shipment in tow.

The Russians aren't only at the mall, it transpires. Joyce, who is unduly worried by the lack of magnetism that she's discovered, speculates that the demagnetisation might come from the now-abandoned lab run until recently

"Will Byers senses from afar that the dreaded Mind Flayer is back – and is, disturbingly, as actively malevolent as ever!"

by Doctors Brenner and Owens. Heading over to the old place, the duo of Joyce and Hopper encounter a Russian soldier called Grigori (Andrey Ivchenko), who attacks Hopper.

Billy, who is mentally enslaved by the Upside Down, and

his workmate Heather, who has also fallen under the spell of the unpleasant rat-creature, are apparently recruiting for the occult cause. They visit Heather's parents, where Max and Eleven drop in to meet them; after those two leave, Billy and Heather subdue poor old Mom and Dad.

From afar, Will Byers senses that this has happened, realising, to his horror, that this is the dreaded work of the Mind Flayer, who is as actively malevolent as ever.

CHAPTER FOUR:
THE SAUNA TEST

The evil mill is now the centre of operations for the Mind

Flayer, who has taken on a physical form, if an unpleasant one – it's made up of flesh from all the exploded rats. Billy and Heather bring the latter's parents to it, where it possesses them, bringing its army of controlled humans to four. This doesn't bode well.

Escaping from their encounter with Grigori, Hopper and Joyce visit the mayor of Hawkins, Larry Kline (Cary Elwes of *Saw* and *The Princess Bride*), based on Hopper's recollection that he once saw Kline and Grigori together. Under pressure, Kline eventually admits that Starcourt Mall is nothing but a front for the Russians, who are buying up abandoned properties across the town for their own nefarious purposes.

Indeed, Starcourt is becoming less and less welcoming: when Dustin, Steve and Robin – accompanied by Lucas Sinclair's sister Erica (Priah Ferguson) – visit the mall, they discover that the loading dock that leads inside is actually an elevator. It traps them beneath the mall which, while worrying, does at least put them in a position to explore the shady goings-on down there.

And 'shady' is the key adjective here, because the town of Hawkins is now subject to all sorts of strange occurrences. After she and Jonathan are fired by their boss, who happens to be Heather's father, for harassing Mrs Driscoll one too many times, Nancy sneaks over to the hospital where the elderly lady is incarcerated. Before her eyes, Mrs D becomes possessed by the Mind Flayer.

At the same time, Will explains to Mike, Lucas, Eleven, and Max, that he has developed a mental connection to the monster and they agree that Billy's actions can only mean that he is enslaved to the creature. They attempt to trap him in the sauna at the swimming pool to demonstrate this – remember, the Mind Flayer likes the cold – but he breaks out, highly aggrieved and clearly

Below: (From left to right) Will, Lucas, Dustin and Max watch as Eleven and Mike saunter off for a pubescent-styled kissing sesh.

99

planning to murder the lot of them. Fortunately, Eleven steps in and overpowers him with telekinesis, pinning him down with a barbell.

Later, Billy returns to the mill – where we witness a whole crowd of possessed Hawkins townsfolk. Oh dear...

CHAPTER FIVE:
THE FLAYED

Multiple storylines are now ongoing, with the overall braid – as they call it in the movies – adding up to a thrilling web of supernatural action. In this episode, the primary arc belongs to Hopper and Joyce, who search through one of the abandoned properties mentioned in Kline's confession.

What do they find? A hidden lab belonging to the Soviets! Chased down by the relentless Grigori, they manage to get away, taking a Russian scientist named Alexei (Alec Utgoff) along as hostage. He doesn't speak English, and Hopper and Joyce certainly don't speak Russian, so they take him to Murray Bauman, our old conspiracy-theory buddy, because Murray happens to speak the language.

Meanwhile, Dustin, Steve, Robin and Erica also find a Russian lab, this time underneath Starcourt Mall, where they witness soldiers unloading boxes of some unknown material from the elevator. While searching for a radio room in order to call for help, they stumble across a massive room where Soviet boffins are doing what we thought they were doing this entire time – trying to open a portal to the Upside Down. Could there be a worse idea than that?

In one of their periodic group get-togethers, Nancy, Jonathan, Will, Mike, Lucas, Eleven and Max come up with the idea that Billy and the fertiliser-chomping Mrs Driscoll have been possessed by the Mind Flayer. Once possessed, they're recruiting more people to be 'flayed' – or mentally enslaved – in order to create an army that will battle on behalf of the Upside Down. They're attacked by two of the Flayed, and although Nancy and Jonathan manage to kill them, they turn into a grisly mass that looks like the Mind Flayer itself.

CHAPTER SIX:
E PLURIBUS UNUM

In between all the occult action, Eleven and Mike are undergoing a Ross-and-Rachel-style on-off romance, never quite getting together and never quite parting ways either. You can't help but root for the couple, who deserve a bit of happiness after all they've been through.

Or should we say, 'are going through', because there's no let-up whatsoever in the endless barrage of life-threatening occurrences in Hawkins. Things seem to be going well as this episode begins, with Eleven incapacitating the Mind Flayer to the extent that it retreats back to its nest at the old mill. Steve and Robin, who have been caught by the Russians in the lab underneath Starcourt Mall and interrogated, are rescued by Dustin and Erica.

Moreover, Murray's grasp of Russian has come in handy because he's translated the words of Hopper and Joyce's hostage Alexei, who confirms that his Russian colleagues are actively trying to get into the Upside Down via the portal they're constructing beneath Starcourt. Hopper calls our old chum Dr Owens and asks him to warn the government about the clandestine Soviet incursion, although – as all sci-fi fans know – you can never trust the government. We are reminded of this one more time when Hawkins' corrupt mayor Larry Kline is approached by the Soviet agent Grigori, who wants him to find Hopper and hand him over.

It's time to confront the Mind Flayer before it overtakes the entire town and maybe even our entire dimension, so Eleven communicates via telepathy with its prime ambassador Billy. In doing so we learn that the lad had a miserable childhood, and we gain a bit of sympathy for him, but there's little time for kissing and making up because Billy tells the Mind Flayer where Eleven is.

It's apparent that the Mind Flayer wants Eleven dead in revenge for destroying the original gate under the old lab, and in due course a horde of Flayed gather at the mill, merging with their boss in one giant, monstrous figure. You really wouldn't want to annoy it, but unfortunately, Eleven already has.

CHAPTER SEVEN:
THE BITE

We're heading rapidly towards the most dramatic season conclusion yet, with multiple storylines resolved – or not, as the case may be – and the fates of many much-loved characters in the balance. In this penultimate episode, the gang know that a showdown between the Mind Flayer and Eleven is imminent, and indeed it happens suddenly, leaving our heroine seriously injured and the kids just about escaping the monster before it kills them all.

The Mind Flayer isn't the only adversary, of course, with a whole brigade of Russian scientists and soldiers for the Hawkins residents to deal with – those Hawkins residents who haven't been turned into an army of the practically undead, of course. Dustin, Erica, Steve and Robin take refuge in the cinema at Starcourt Mall, while Eleven's group just want one thing – to help her recover from the injury she sustained while battling the Mind Flayer. They hole up in a supermarket to gather supplies, where Dustin contacts them over walkie-talkie to inform them of what's going on at the mall. In due course, they all gather at Starcourt, where the final confrontation is set to take place.

It's all looking pretty bleak. Hopper's team search everywhere for the kids, winding up at a fairground where they are seen by the unreliable mayor, Kline. He tells the Russians where they are, and in due course the soldiers track Hopper down. The scientist, Alexei, is shot dead by Grigori, and it looks as if the same fate awaits the rest of them, despite a brilliant diversionary tactic by Murray, who confuses their attackers by speaking Russian to them.

Eleven is in a bad way by now – and although her group arrives at the mall and saves Dustin from being shot by the Russians, her energy is spent and she collapses. We zoom in for a look at the wound she sustained in the fight with the Mind Flayer: there's something very unusual about it.

Left: (From left to right) Will, Lucas, El, Mike, Max, Jonathan and Nancy discover another entrance to the Upside Down.

Bottom Left: Misogynistic Hawkins Post journalist Bruce Lowe gets his comeuppance by the end of season three.

> "The final episode is an object lesson in how to write a compelling conclusion and wring emotions out of every scene"

CHAPTER EIGHT:
THE BATTLE OF STARCOURT

The final episode of season three of *Stranger Things* is an object lesson in how to write a compelling conclusion and wring emotions, good and bad, out of every scene. We really need ten pages to analyse it fully, but let's just say that this excellent chunk of TV revolves around the concept of self-sacrifice for the greater good.

Cleverly, the writers immediately remove any expectations we may have had that this season is going to end with yet another climactic scene of Eleven versus monster, in which she defeats her adversary with her telekinetic strength. Far from it: as the episode opens, she uses her powers to blast open her wound and eject the piece of Mind Flayer that was stuck in it. While this is undoubtedly the sensible thing to do, the move also removes her mental powers completely: after this, she can't even crush a can of Coke with telekinesis, let alone take on a skyscraper-sized monster.

So who's going to defeat the Mind Flayer? Read on...

After many manoeuvres, the team find themselves at the gate constructed by the Soviets to the Upside Down. Earlier, Alexei told them how to explode the gate, the building and the Mind Flayer – if only they can do it without blowing themselves up too. Standing between them and victory are Billy and Grigori; although she has no telekinetic

powers, Eleven can still communicate telepathically, and she reminds Billy of the childhood love of his mother, which snaps him out of the Mind Flayer's mental control. Apologising to his sister Max for his behaviour, Billy delays the monster's attack by sacrificing himself.

As for Grigori, it's time for Jim Hopper to show his quality: he fights and defeats the *Terminator*-like Russian, but in doing so gets trapped in the very machinery that they're trying to destroy. With no other option, and time running out because the Mind Flayer is preparing to deliver a final blow, he nods to Joyce to destroy the gate. In tears, she complies – and the massive explosion destroys the gate, the soldiers, and apparently Hopper (crushing any hopes fans had for a Jim-Joyce romance). The cavalry arrives in the form of Dr Owens plus American soldiers, as the Mind Flayer dies.

We cut to three months later. Starcourt is no more. The multiple deaths, including those of the Flayed, have been attributed to the mall's destruction. Kline has been disgraced and arrested. The Byers family, with whom the still-powerless Eleven now lives, are on the point of

moving to California, and who can blame them? Mike and Eleven finally declare their love for each other and plan to meet at Thanksgiving.

So that's it, then? Everything's all right now?

Come on, you know better than that. This is *Stranger Things*, after all, and in a mid-credits scene we're taken briefly to Kamchatka in Russia. In a grim government facility, guards are ordered to feed a prisoner to a full-sized captive Demogorgon – but "not the American", they're told. Hooper, is that you?

Looks like season four is going to have some surprises...

Above: Dustin (left) and Steve (right) get down to business deciphering Russian radio transmissions at Ships Ahoy!

Right: El protects the gang by harnessing her anger to wreak unstoppable power upon their enemies.

SEASON FOUR AND BEYOND

BUCKLE UP FOR FRESH, SCARY & MYSTERIOUS HAPPENINGS AS A NEW VILLAIN EMERGES FROM THE UPSIDE DOWN

Further on screen thrills seemed guaranteed after the Duffer Brothers signed a nine-figure deal with Netflix - that's at least $100 million by the way – and delivered the scripts for their most ambitious season yet in September 2019.

Filming began in early 2020 but then a real life horror – a global pandemic - brought proceedings screeching to a halt as production shut down during the Covid-19 lockdowns, meaning fans had to wait three years for their next fix!

When nine new episodes eventually dropped in two volumes on 27 May and 1 July 2022 they did not disappoint, nor pull any punches. The season was the biggest yet, both in terms of the scope of its content, the length of its episodes, and the expansion of its cast. This being a highly creative premise, new characters were introduced to spice up the action, including metalhead Eddie Munson (Joseph Quinn), entitled jock Jason Carver (Mason Dye) and Upside Down monster Vecna (Jamie Campbell Bower).

Above: El in training to regain her powers

107

Fans were also excited to spot Robert Englund as the mysterious Victor Creel and Tom Wlaschiha as prison guard Enzo. The former, in case you've never heard of him, is the veteran actor who originated from the role of Freddy Krueger in the utterly terrifying Nightmare on Elm Street movie series in the Eighties, while Tom Wlaschiha tore up the screen in Game of Thrones.

Three days after it was launched, the series smashed all records for viewer numbers.

For the first time since Eleven went to meet Kali in Chicago in season two, the action moves out of Indiana. We already knew that we would see the Byers family in California where they had relocated - presumably in search of better weather and fewer demonic attacks than they've been getting in Hawkins since 1983 – but

what we didn't know was that we were also going to Russia. Russia? Yes, because the cliff hanger of season three, which saw Jim Hopper vanish in a giant explosion, was resolved. The good news - he's alive! - was swiftly followed by the bad; he's imprisoned far from home in a Russian labour camp facing dangers both human... and other. Not so great for him, but fantastic news for fans because Stranger Things without Jim Hopper would be a bit like an Iron Maiden concert in the daytime: way less dark, but also way less fun.

Clearly inspired by classic horror films from the 1970s and 80s, the new episodes are definitely darker and see several character deaths, with narrow escapes and blindingly shocking developments for others.

HERE'S A WHISTLESTOP RECAP....

Above: Dustin, Eddie and Mike share a joke in chapter one, The Hellfire Club

Right: Dungeon Master Eddie Munson, strikes a devil pose

CHAPTER ONE:
THE HELLFIRE CLUB

The action begins with a flashback to Dr Brennan's lab in 1979 when a mysterious incident kills all the test subjects, except Eleven. It appears that she's responsible – but we'll come back to this!

We then skip to the 'present day' of 1986, some six months after the Battle of Starcourt, to find Joyce and her sons settling into their new lives in California, while Eleven, who moved with them, is struggling with the loss of her powers and being bullied at Leonora High School. Back in Hawkins, Mike and Dustin have also moved up to High School, where they join Hellfire, the Dungeons & Dragons club, run by new character Eddie Munson.

When Joyce receives a porcelain doll in the mail, seemingly from Russia, and finds a hidden note stating that Hopper is alive she knows that she must go and find him.

Meanwhile, new character Chrissy Cunningham, captain of the cheerleaders, is being plagued by visions of her family and a grandfather clock. While with Eddie one day she is possessed and killed by a creature from her visions – it's the season's new villain Vecna of course. It's not clear at this point, but Vecna is sentient and able to kill from the Upside Down, finding his way in through feelings of shame and guilt in his victims. Eddie, who's witnessed the whole thing, is naturally freaked out in one of the best series premieres ever!

CHAPTER TWO:
VECNA'S CURSE

In another illuminating flashback, we see how Hopper survived the explosion underneath Starcourt Mall, only to be captured by Russian soldiers and taken to a prison camp in Kamchatka. Downer! Back to 1986 and, working with PI Murray Bauman, Joyce makes contact with one of Hopper's prison guards who tells her to bring US$40,000 dollars to Alaska to get Hopper back.

During a visit to California, Mike heads out roller skating with Will and Eleven and witness' her total humiliation by class bully Angela. Severely provoked and unable to retaliate with her powers, Eleven hits Angela in the face with a roller skate. There's a lot of blood!

Back in Hawkins, having heard from Max that Eddie ran away the night of Chrissy's murder, Dustin, Robin and Steve go to find their new friend and believe his protestations of innocence. They tell him about The Upside Down and together they work out that Vecna killed Chrissy. Further bad news for Eddie is that Chrissy's boyfriend Jason blames him for her murder, branding the Hellfire Club a Satanic cult.

Student reporter Nancy and her sidekick Fred begin their own investigation into Chrissy's death, discovering that a Hawkins resident called Victor Creel, institutionalised for murdering his family back in the 1950s, could be responsible. Before he can act on the information, Fred is murdered by Vecna in the woods in the same manner as Chrissy – body levitated, with limbs snapping and eyes sickeningly popping.

CHAPTER THREE:
THE MONSTER AND THE SUPERHERO

After the roller skate head-bashing, Eleven is arrested but escapes, rescued by Sam Owens whose plan to restore her powers convinces her to go with him. Joyce and Murray's secret adventures continue as they travel to Alaska to drop off Hopper's ransom. Nancy and Robin discover that Victor Creel blamed his family's murders

Above: Vecna controls his world

111

on a demon and work out it is Vecna. They're not the only amateur investigators! Max does some sleuthing of her own and discovers that Chrissy and Fred both suffered from PTSD and experienced other weird physical symptoms like hers. She then hears Vecna call her name and has the grandfather clock vision.

CHAPTER FOUR:
DEAR BILLY

This show-stopper episode is among the best ever - a tour de force for Max, taking a central role this season as she struggles to get over Billy's death. Fearing that Vecna is about to kill her, she goes to the cemetery and as she

sits by Billy's gravestone she is indeed possessed by Vecna and finds herself at an altar inside his mind. Now understanding that music can break Vecna's spell, Steve, Dustin, and Lucas play Max her favourite song, Running Up That Hill by Kate Bush, which opens a portal so that she can narrowly escape. It's a highlight of the season for fans – and of course for Kate Bush who in real life has a huge hit with her 37-year-old song.

In other news, Nancy and Robin interview Victor Creel in prison, who tells them of his family's deathly brush with supernatural forces. And there's bad luck for Joyce and Murray who deliver the ransom money to Russian smuggler and go-between Yuri, only to be betrayed by him. Hopper, who had escaped the prison camp, is recaptured.

Above: Eleven poses for a police mug shot after being arrested for the skate attack.

Above: Max under
Vecna's control

Back at the Byers house, where Jonathan was in charge of Mike and Will while Joyce was away, bodyguards sent by Owens now rule the roost, monitoring things as a new government faction, led by new character Lt Colonel Sullivan, is also after Eleven. As they are being watched by Sam Owen's agents, Jonathan, Mike, and Will escape from an attack on their home by armed soldiers, helped by new character Argyle. They end up bringing Agent Harmon with them after he's been shot.

CHAPTER FIVE:
THE NINA PROJECT

With the title begging the question, who or what is Nina, Dr Brenner is back! Turns out that Nina is a computer programme linked to a specialised isolation tank he's developed with Owens in Nevada to help Eleven access memories of her time as a child at Hawkins Lab.

Back in California, and injured Agent Harmon, realising he's not long for this world, gives the boys a number for the NINA project which connects to a modem. Needing help in making a connection, Mike enlists the help of Dustin's girlfriend Suzie in Salt Lake City.

In Russia, we find Hopper back in prison, now alongside his old guard Antonov. While flying to Russia, Joyce and

Murray overpower the double-crossing Yuri but crash-land in the wilderness in the process.

Max, Lucas, Steve, and Dustin regroup with Nancy and Robin and check out the Creel house, encountering flickering lights (flashback to episode one) which they trace to Vecna's movements beneath the house in the Upside Down.

But they don't stop Vecna managing a third killing – this time it's Patrick, a friend of Jason who was helping him chase Eddie.

CHAPTER SIX:
THE DIVE

In all three plot strands the good guys are now closing in on their foes. With Suzie coming up trumps in locating the NINA project, the California kids are closer to finding Eleven, the Hawkins gang is at the point of facing Vecna, and Joyce and Murray are battling with Yuri to try and break Hopper out of prison. As if life wasn't tough enough there, Hopper is now about to fight a Demogorgon – can no one give this guy a break?

Working with Dr 'Papa' Brenner to restore her powers, Eleven comes to believe (wrongly as it turns out) that she was responsible for the lab massacre.

Back in Hawkins, Steve's group manage to track down Eddie who's in hiding since becoming a 'person of interest' to the police and hated by the townsfolk after Jason convinced everyone that he's a vessel for Satan.

They also trace a new gate to the Upside Down, in nearby Lover's Lake. When Steve dives down to inspect it he is yanked inside and attacked by Demobats, so naturally (!) Nancy, Robin, and Eddie go in after him.

CHAPTER SEVEN:
THE MASSACRE AT HAWKINS LAB

The volume one finale is a cracker, explaining a lot about the show's mythology and setting up huge cliff hangers.

Joyce, Murray, and Yuri manage to get into the prison in time to help Hopper escape the Demogorgon and then the prison. Joyce and Hopper reunite (I'm not crying, you are).

Dustin, Lucas, and his sister and new gang member Erica, theorise that Vecna has a gate at the site of each murder. They manage to let Steve's group in the Upside Down know and they make their escape through the Creel house above, which is discovered to be frozen in time – it's still 1983 in fact, when the series began. Robin and Eddie get out and regroup with the others inside Eddie's trailer at the gate where Chrissy died. But Nancy isn't so lucky and gets possessed by Vecna who, arrogantly shows her something of his real history. She discovers he is Victor

Above: Papa's children

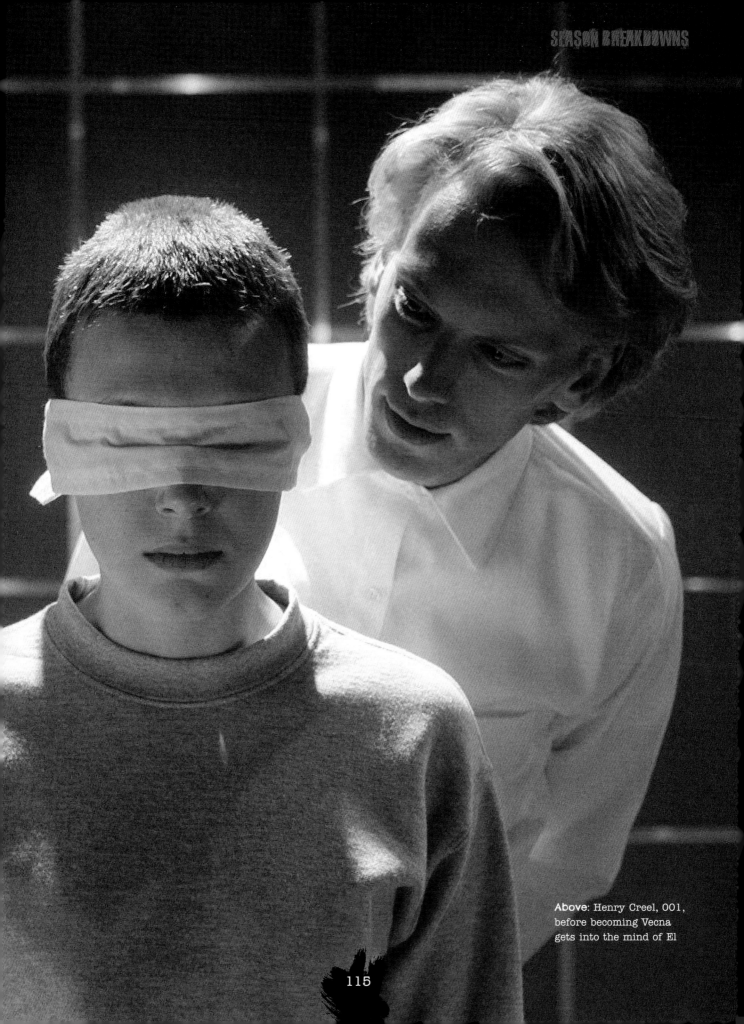

Above: Henry Creel, 001, before becoming Vecna gets into the mind of El

Above: Enzo, Murray, Joyce and Hopper

Creel's son Henry, who killed his mother and sister with his psychokinetic powers before falling into a coma and being placed in Brenner's care as test subject 001. Shocker!

Eleven eventually remembers Henry committing the lab massacre and trying to kill her when she refused to help. The final moments of the episode reveal that after overpowering Henry in an ensuing fight, Eleven sent him to the Upside Down, where he became the monstrous Vecna. This important information about Vecna's backstory and true identity can surely only help our heroes as they continue the fight in volume two.

Hawkins. But her escape is thwarted by Brenner who is determined that Eleven completes her training – he's been using her all these years to try to get to Henry in the Upside Down. Just as Brenner has recaptured her, Lt Colonel Sullivan and his forces arrive at the site. Although they had planned to kill her, their arrival is actually good luck as it allows her to escape from Brenner who gets shot in the ensuing melee.

Eleven uses her powers to take Sullivan's soldiers out, just as Mike's group arrives. Reunited with Jonathan and the others, the group is back together and begins a desperate 2,000 mile trip back to Hawkins.

CHAPTER EIGHT:
PAPA

The story picks up in volume two, with Vecna giving Nancy a terrifying vision of the future showing Hawkins underneath a dark cloud, torn apart by rifts and descended on by monsters. He then releases her.

Having worked out that Vecna needs one more gate to enact his plan, Max offers to lure Vecna into possessing her so the others can attack him while he is distracted. In the lab Eleven has regained her powers and, learning of her friends' plan, gets Owens to arrange her return to

CHAPTER NINE:
THE PIGGYBACK

It's all hands on deck as the various groups begin to enact their plans.

Max, Lucas and Erica go to the Creel House while Steve, Nancy and Robin go to the Upside Down beneath to attack Vecna. Dustin and Eddie are charged with drawing away the Demobats – no easy task and poor Eddie pays with his life.

Realising that they physically cannot get back in time, Eleven's group make another plan. They manage to create an isolation tank to allow Eleven to fight Vecna by 'piggybacking' and entering Max's mind. Their plan succeeds until Eleven is eventually overwhelmed by Vecna who manages to possess Max nevertheless.

But all is not lost. After the big question of saying 'I love you' has loomed over the couple throughout the season, Mike eventually says those three little words to Eleven, which gives her the strength to break Vecna's control over Max.

While she's unable to stop Max dying for a minute from her injuries, Eleven does manage to revive her enough that she goes into a coma.

Hopper, Joyce and Murray realise that their best way of helping is by re-entering the prison and killing the remaining Demogorgons, to weaken Vecna's powers.

So it's a two-pronged attack, with Steve, Robin and Nancy attacking Vecna's physical form with flames and bullets, as the others set about diluting the powers of his mind. He is left apparently dead.

But things don't look good otherwise. Max lays in a coma having lost her sight and with every one of her limbs broken, plus Vecna was able to use the time of her brief death to open his gates and tear through Hawkins causing devastation which is sold to the town's blissfully ignorant population as an earthquake.

This whole crazy action-packed double bill finale ran to nearly four hours – phew. In the final moments, the calm after the storm, all the central characters reunite. But in a foreboding final scene Will senses Vecna is still alive and the Upside Down begins invading Hawkins......

Above: Eddie shreds in the name of diversion in Season 4's The Piggyback

Above: An emotional end for Eddie as Dustin shares his last breaths in Season 4's The Piggyback

TEASER FOR
SEASON FIVE

Enjoying this epic collection of Stranger Things-related wisdom? Well, even when you've finished reading, the fun won't stop – because season five is on the way. As we go to press, the new season hasn't been written, so we can't tell you exactly what to expect, but even if we could, where would be the fun in that? Right now we're having a whale of a time speculating about what might happen as we look forward to our fifth go-around in the coolest sci-fi universe in years.

The fifth and final (what!?) season of Stranger Things was officially announced on 17 February 2022 and is expected to drop mid-2024. The two-hour long final episode was so fantastic that we were left wondering where on earth (or Upside Down) the series could possibly go? Of course the Duffer Brothers have known for years. They planned

out the final series while still writing season four and it's hinted that it involves a global disaster.

The brothers have also teased eight episodes and said that on average they won't be as 'extreme' in length as the ones produced for season four. The exception to that rule will be the season finale which is set to be 'pretty massive' . They have also promised a return to fewer locations and a simpler structure, more like the first season, but bigger in scale and scope.

As 'un-psychic' mortals, we don't yet know about the fictional timeline and setting, other than, in line with the previous four seasons, there will be a time jump – probably more pronounced than before to reflect the fact that the cast of younger actors are now grown up and looking older than their character ages.

Above: Things are not looking good for Hawkins

As far as we know pretty much everyone is coming back for season five. Why any actor would quit a show as successful as Stranger Things is beyond us.

The plot remains a mystery for now, although the Duffer Brothers have said that they will flesh out the demonic underworld even more as 'a lot of those answers for the Upside Down is really what the basis of season five is about'. There are also suggestions that the brothers might take some real risks and plot 'the unthinkable'. Critics believe the Duffer's decision to allow all the central cast members to survive the 'unsurvivable' can't go on.

We have to wait to see whether Eleven will fully regain her powers, and whether Max will come out of her coma? What about Will? How will his key relationships with Mike, Dustin and Lucas evolve as the boys become men?

Then there's Joyce, who we can all agree deserves a shot at happiness. Will she settle down with Hopper, who has serious issues of his own to deal with, including the lingering trauma of his daughter's death: do characters like his ever really find peace? We'd like to think so, but we're not optimistic.

Despite all the action of the season four finale, we are left with many questions about the characters, the fate of Hawkins, and the predicted return of Vecna.

Got a theory of your own?
Let us know!

SEE YOU FOR SEASON 5!

Above: Eleven gets the Funko Pop! Vinyl treatment – note the trademark nosebleed and Eggos.

A WORLD TURNED UPSIDE DOWN

HOW STRANGER THINGS CONQUERED PLANET EARTH, VIA SPIN-OFFS, MERCHANDISE AND MORE

Politicians aren't traditionally known for leading the way when it comes to popular culture, so when a lawmaker references a hit movie or TV show, you know it's truly been absorbed into public consciousness. *Stranger Things* had its crossover moment in February 2017 when David Cicilline, a Democrat Congressman in the US House of Representatives, made an unfavourable comparison between President Donald Trump's administration and the show's freaky parallel dimension. "Like the main characters in *Stranger Things*," he said, "we are now stuck in the Upside Down."

Just as President Ronald Reagan had when he channelled *Back to the Future* in his 1986 State of the Union address – shamelessly ripping off Doc Brown's iconic "where we're going, we don't need roads" line – Cicilline's remarks made it clear that in just a few short months, the Duffer Brothers' story of weird-goings-on in a small Indiana town had captured the zeitgeist. Ironically, a show built around its homages to the pop culture of a bygone age was now the hottest thing in town, becoming a cultural landmark in its own right.

The show's influence would go on to stretch way beyond politicians' watch-lists, however. Thanks to Eleven's love of Eggos, the Kellogg's-manufactured brand of waffles saw a spike in demand and – while the company wasn't involved in the first run of episodes – they'd go on to supply an '80s-vintage ad for season two's Super Bowl commercial. Coca-Cola also briefly resurrected its controversial New Coke flavour – which had proved so unpopular on its original 1985 launch that it was pulled after 79 days – as part of a third-season tie-in.

Now firmly established alongside *The Witcher*, *Bridgerton* and, well, *The Crown* as one of the jewels in the Netflix crown, *Stranger Things* has spawned a multimedia empire of tie-in novels, games, toys and more to become one of the biggest popular culture brands in this – or any other – dimension.

#STRANGERTHINGS

When *Stranger Things* debuted in 2016, the accepted wisdom was that the era of watercooler television – the kind of shows that get everyone talking in the office, pub or playground – was coming to an end. In contrast to the 20th century, when linear broadcast schedules ruled the TV landscape, the chances of getting everyone watching at the same time – as they would when *The X-Files* or *Frasier* ruled – were slim, as people instead followed their own viewing schedules, crafting bespoke watchlists to suit their tastes on their streaming services of choice.

Within days of its launch, however, it was clear that *Stranger Things* had the power to get *everyone* talking. If you had seen it, you felt duty-bound to spread the word, and if you were yet to watch it, you had to catch up as quickly as humanly possible to ensure you didn't pick up a massive spoiler about Will Byers' fate, or the secrets of Eleven's past.

Inevitably, social media exploded with conversation about Netflix's new hit series, and sometimes in the most unpredictable ways. When the Duffer brothers dreamed up and wrote the part of Hawkins High School student Barbara Holland, for example, she was very much a supporting player, the sort of character who usually appears in a couple of episodes before being consigned to a file marked "forgotten guest star".

But after she was abducted and killed by a Demogorgon, sending best friend Nancy Wheeler on an ultimately fruitless missing-persons investigation, she became the subject of a cause célèbre online, driven by the #JusticeForBarb and #WeAreAllBarb hashtags. The unexpectedly vocal fan response would subsequently impact the show's second season, as the Duffers added a storyline about Nancy's anger over the town's indifference to her friend's death.

"I remember directing Barb's death in the Upside Down swimming pool, and [Shannon Purser] was a young actress who had done almost nothing [beforehand] – I think she still had a part-time job at a movie theatre selling popcorn," recalled executive producer/director

Left: A pair of fans cosplay Steve and Robin, aka Scoops Ahoy's finest, at Los Angeles Comic-Con.

Shawn Levy ahead of the second season. "I kept apologising that she had to be covered in slime and climb these disgusting vines. And she was in heaven, she was like, 'Are you kidding me? This is a blast!' So to see that same hard-working, humble, cheerful young woman become a cultural icon was shocking... and incredibly fun."

For the performers higher up the call sheet, *Stranger Things* made casting directors sit up and take notice, as one of those rare productions – like *Four Weddings and a Funeral*, *Trainspotting* and *The Lord of the Rings* – that has the power to turn actors into stars. As the nominal face of the show, Millie Bobby Brown became one of the most in-demand teen actors on the planet, and the young Brit was soon headlining the blockbuster likes of *Godzilla: King of the Monsters* and Netflix's own *Enola Holmes*.

Her surrogate screen dad, David Harbour (Chief Hopper), meanwhile, quickly said goodbye to the background player credits that had previously dominated his career,

donning some hefty red prosthetics to headline the *Hellboy* reboot, and – most high-profile of all – play the Red Guardian opposite Scarlett Johansson in *Black Widow*. Even the stars who weren't set to trouble the A-list found their lives changed forever, as the cast became regulars on red carpets, as well as star attractions at comic-cons.

That said, the show's influence was soon evident across Hollywood. So while *IT: Chapter One* was in production before *Stranger Things* launched – and the original Stephen King book was, itself, an influence on the show – it's probable that the teen-focused, '80s-set Pennywise adaptation got a leg-up at the box office from some common themes. And in 2021, the wonderful *Ghostbusters: Afterlife* gave the franchise a Hawkins-flavoured reboot, basing the story around kids in small-town America. We're sure it's just a coincidence that both films feature *Stranger Things* star Finn Wolfhard...

A WIDER WORLD

Perhaps the cruellest thing about *Stranger Things* is that, since it dropped on Netflix nearly six years ago, we've only been treated to 25 episodes. For a fanbase hungry for more stories, that's precious little to cling onto, but thankfully – in the tradition of *Star Wars*, *Star Trek* and *Doctor Who* – there's plenty of expanded universe material to plunge your teeth into.

If you want to know more about the story behind the show, the official companion book, *Worlds Turned Upside Down* by Gina McIntyre, weaves interviews with the creative team together with plenty of artwork to show how the Duffers brothers' grand nostalgic vision coalesced. Netflix also produced a *Talking Dead*-style after show to accompany season two, in which *Community*'s dean, Jim Rash, chatted with cast and crew to dissect key elements of the plot.

Perhaps more interesting for hardcore fans, however, are the new stories being told within the universe, designed to enhance the backstories of key characters in the show. In the first *Stranger Things* novel, *Suspicious Minds* (published in February 2019, a few months ahead of season three's launch), author Gwenda Bond headed back to the late '60s to tell the story of Eleven's mother, Terry, and the morally dubious experiments that gave her daughter telekinetic powers. In it, Dr Brenner – the scientist played by Matthew Modine – emerges as an antagonist every bit as creepy as the Mind Flayer, while the story gains extra poignancy once you're aware of Terry's sad fate in the saga.

"It's definitely a look at Eleven's origin story," Bond explained ahead of the book's release. "My goal was to tell a story that would help people better understand and fall in love with Terry Ives as a hero in her own right – albeit a tragic one – and deepen their connection to the show.

"The whole *Stranger Things* writing team gave me a brilliantly wide remit to put my own stamp on the story," she added. "Paul [Dichter, the creative consultant] would run back and forth on the set running bits of story by the Duffers, making sure there were no spoilers as we went along. But with other things they allowed me to add my own unique ideas not covered in the show, like the backstory for Eleven's dad."

Suspicious Minds was soon followed by Adam Christopher's *Darkness on the Edge of Town*, in which Chief Hopper tells Eleven about his experiences as a New York cop in the late '70s – a past that's been alluded to but never really explored on screen.

"The first supernatural thing that Hopper ever experiences takes place in season one of the TV show, and here I am writing a story that's set years before," Christopher told a recent issue of *SFX* magazine. "The question was, 'How do you write a *Stranger Things* story that doesn't have any of that stuff in it?' Because when someone's walking into a bookstore, they're going to want a *Stranger Things* story.

"The TV show is full of '80s stuff," he continued, "so I loaded the book with period detail from '70s New York. Then I had to come up with a story that was not only *Stranger Things*, but didn't contradict the TV show. We kind of left it open. Does the antagonist have supernatural powers or was it actually just something else? It was great because the showrunners,

Left: Does San Diego Comic-Con have an Upside Down? A fan becomes a strangely endearing Demogorgon.

Below: Adam Christopher's *Darkness on the Edge of Town* on sale – a name inspired by a Bruce Springsteen album.

the producers and the publisher trusted that I could come up with something that fitted with what they wanted."

With a further novel focusing on Max Mayfield's life before she joined the ensemble, as well as numerous Dark Horse graphic novels and *Beyond Hawkins* – a six-part prequel podcast featuring Scoops Ahoy Employee of the Year Robin Buckley – the original TV show is apparently now just the tip of a vast *Stranger Things* iceberg. In fact, TV spin-offs may even be on the cards after the Duffers used the recent announcement that the show's fifth season will be its last to tease that, "There are still many more exciting stories to tell within the world of *Stranger Things*: new mysteries, new adventures, new unexpected heroes..."

HAWKINS BAZAAR

If there's a strong argument that pop culture entities haven't really arrived until they've been immortalised in some brand of plastic bricks, then at least *Stranger Things*

5

can say it's followed in the rather large footsteps of *Star Wars*, *Harry Potter* and the Marvel Cinematic Universe. Lego's 2,287-piece Upside Down set (now, sadly, retired) is an ingenious creation that features both the normal Hawkins and its twisted, decaying reflection. You can also find yourself a surprisingly cute Demogorgon keyring, and both Eleven and a Demogorgon replicated in the distinctive blocky form of the BrickHeadz line.

Then again, there's no shortage of quirky representations of the *Stranger Things* regulars out there. Funko's Pop! Vinyl figures are arguably even more ubiquitous than Lego, and Eleven, Hopper and the rest have been given the range's big-headed, facial feature-lite treatment. McFarlane Toys, meanwhile, have run the characters through the ultra-cute, anime-esque filter of their Q posket series. (And if you just want a standard realistic action figure with the usual points of articulation, fear not – McFarlane have a licence for those too.)

GAMER THINGS

For those looking for something a little more interactive, you'll be pleased to hear that games are also a major part of the *Stranger Things* rights bonanza.

Dungeons & Dragons has been integral to *Stranger Things* since day one, acting as much of an influence on the Duffers as Stephen King and *The Goonies*: Mike, Dustin, Lucas and Will are big fans – the question of whether to play or explore 'cooler' pursuits becomes a source of tension within the gang during later seasons – while Upside Down residents the Demogorgons and the Mind Flayer are named after monsters in the long-running fantasy role-playing game.

It feels appropriate, then, that D&D owners Wizards of the Coast (a subsidiary of Hasbro) released a *Stranger Things*-themed version of the game back in 2019. The

Left: Justice for Barb! Actor Shannon Purser gatecrashes *Stranger Things* Hall H panel at San Diego Comic-Con 2017.

starter set allows you to play as one of five characters inspired by the TV show (Mike is a paladin, for example, while Eleven is, rather appropriately, a wizard), and the story is based on the Hunt for the Thessalhydra adventure the boys were playing in season one – before Will found himself otherwise engaged in the Upside Down, that is.

And if you prefer your boardgames to be more financial than fantastical, Hasbro has released a *Stranger Things* Monopoly set, which transfers the eternally popular cause of numerous family arguments to Hawkins and the Upside Down. Eighties-appropriate playing pieces include an Eggo waffle, a skateboard and a walkie-talkie (baby Demogorgon Dart takes the place of the ever-popular dog), while the game adds some new twists on an old formula, with bike and station wagon squares allowing players to tunnel under the town.

Now that Netflix has launched a gaming section on its platform, it's no surprise that a pair of *Stranger Things*-themed titles were part of the launch slate. *Stranger Things: 1984* reimagines the key locations of Hawkins in 8-bit-style graphics that riff on the arcade stylings of the '80s. Each character has a unique skill set, with collecting Eggos a common theme throughout. *Stranger Things 3: The Game*, meanwhile, allows you to play through the events of the third season on your mobile device.

And just to prove that there's nowhere the Upside Down can't touch, *Stranger Things* has crossed over into the likes of *Minecraft*, *Fortnite*, *Dead by Daylight* and *SMITE*.

If Hawkins, Indiana, did shops… A glimpse of the *Stranger Things* pop-up store in New York's Times Square.

BACK IN TIME

If smartphone apps and videogames feel a bit too 21st century for a show set in the '80s, there have also been chances to experience the world of Hawkins in a more traditional, analogue way.

Since 2007, London-based Secret Cinema has specialised in putting on immersive screenings of movie classics, where visitors get to spend a few hours in the worlds of films like *Star Wars: The Empire Strikes Back*, *Back to the Future* and *Alien*. The company's 2019/20 production of *Stranger Things* marked their first foray into television – "the perfect place to launch our TV strand," said founder Fabien Riggall – and guests clad in spandex, huge hair and other mainstays of '80s catwalks got to step out in Hawkins' Starcourt Mall for the town's imaginary Fourth of July celebrations. It was an evening of arcade games, illicit house parties, ice cream from Scoops Ahoy and occasional jaunts to the Upside Down.

Over in the US, Stranger Things: The Experience came to New York and San Francisco in spring/summer 2022. Following a similarly 'don't tell anyone' vibe to Secret Cinema, the event will invite guests to explore Hawkins Lab, teasing that "there may be the occasional testing, analysis, or psych evaluation. Don't worry, it's safe… perfectly safe…" We'll take their word for it… The event's Mix-Tape Area will also provide "a medley of *Stranger Things* locations and fan-favourite moments", including photo ops, *Stranger Things*-inspired food and drink and a bar. Hawkins may be a fictional town, but it's about to get a lot easier to visit.

And for anyone who'd rather not run the risk of running into a Demogorgon in the loos (which is perfectly understandable), you could always settle for rewatching the existing four seasons to get yourself ready for the eagerly anticipated fifth – though if you're a true fan you may want to make sure you're wearing your Stranger Things t-shirt, getting a caffeine injection from your Stranger Things mug, and taking notes in your VHS-style Stranger Things notebook.